The Palace of Versailles

Other titles in the *History's Great Structures* series include:

History's Great
STRUCTURES

The Palace of
Versailles

Craig E. Blohm

ReferencePoint
Press®

San Diego, CA

© 2015 ReferencePoint Press, Inc.
Printed in the United States

For more information, contact:
ReferencePoint Press, Inc.
PO Box 27779
San Diego, CA 92198
www.ReferencePointPress.com

LIBRARY OF CONGRESS CATALOGING-IN-PUBLICATION DATA

Blohm, Craig E., 1948-
  The Palace of Versailles / by Craig E. Blohm.
    pages cm. -- (History's great structures series)
  Includes bibliographical references and index.
  ISBN-13: 978-1-60152-684-7 (hardback)
  ISBN-10: 1-60152-684-9 (hardback)
 1. Château de Versailles (Versailles, France)--History. 2. Versailles (France)--Buildings, structures, etc. 3. France--Kings and rulers--Dwellings. 4. France--Court and courtiers. I. Title.
  DC801.V57B55   2014
  944'.3663--dc23
                                      2013050296

CONTENTS

IMPORTANT EVENTS IN THE HISTORY OF THE PALACE OF VERSAILLES

1638
Louis XIV is born.

1661
The first building campaign at Versailles begins.

1648
The rebellions known as the Frondes begin.

1667
The excavation of the Grand Canal begins.

1623
Construction begins on Louis's hunting lodge.

1600   1635   1670

1631
Construction begins on a château to replace the hunting lodge.

1668
The second building campaign begins.

1610
Louis XIII becomes king.

1656
Construction of Vaux-le-Vicomte begins.

1979
The United Nations Educational, Scientific and Cultural Organization designates Versailles a World Heritage Site.

1678
The third building campaign begins.

1870
The Franco-Prussian War begins.

2013
André Le Nôtre is commemorated on the four-hundredth anniversary of his birth.

1699
The fourth building campaign begins.

1700　　1800　　1900　　2000

1715
Louis XIV dies.

1919
The Treaty of Versailles ends World War I.

1999
Versailles is damaged by a catastrophic storm.

1789
The French Revolution begins.

1682
Louis XIV moves the seat of government to Versailles.

1801
The Museum of Versailles opens.

The Palace of the Sun King

It is perhaps fitting that the word *palace* comes from the Old French term *palais*, meaning "grand residence." For there is no more universally recognized example of an elegant, opulent, and expensive dwelling than France's Palace of Versailles. During its time as a royal residence, Versailles went through periods of large-scale construction that employed tens of thousands of workers but drained massive amounts of money from the French treasury. It also weathered long periods of neglect when funds were needed to fight costly wars. For nearly 170 years Versailles served as the principal home to four kings, before a popular revolution swept through France beginning in 1789 and ultimately destroyed the monarchy. Although each French king left his unique mark on the palace, its grandeur is due in large part to one man: Louis XIV, "the Sun King."

Louis was just four years old when he became king of France upon the death of his father, Louis XIII. Too young to rule the nation, his mother, Anne of Austria, governed France until Louis came of age. Even at birth, Louis had been regarded as special. His father was nearly thirty-seven years old and still had no male child to continue the royal line. After having suffered four miscarriages, Queen Anne finally delivered a healthy boy on September 5, 1638. The long-awaited son and heir to the throne, Louis XIV was hailed as a miracle and called *le dieudonné*, "the God-given child."

A Palace Fit for a King

By the time Louis was twenty-three years old and ready to lead his nation, Paris had been the political and cultural center of France for centuries. As Jean-Baptiste Colbert, Louis XIV's minister of finances, observed, "Paris being the capital of the kingdom and the seat of the King, it is certain that it sets the pace for all the rest of the country."[1] It was also the center of political unrest, a fact that distressed the king. But Louis already had his sights set on another place from which to rule his kingdom. He had grown up spending many enjoyable days at his father's hunting lodge in the small village of Versailles outside of Paris. In Versailles, he saw a place away from the traditional centers of politics where he could establish apartments, or residences, for the noblemen who might oppose his policies or even plot to overthrow him. Keeping a tight rein on those who had political ambitions would allow Louis to suppress any budding opposition. His father had expanded the hunting lodge, transforming it into a modest château. In order to provide the living space necessary for thousands of residents, Louis continued the expansion on a grand scale never seen before. From a humble hunting lodge, the Palace of Versailles eventually grew to become the most magnificent palace in Europe.

WORDS IN CONTEXT
opulent
Displaying great wealth.

The statistics behind the palace are as staggering as the beauty of Versailles itself. Encompassing 721,182 square feet (67,000 sq. m), today the château lies on 2,014 acres (815 ha) of exquisite formal gardens that feature 200,000 trees, 50 fountains, more than 300 marble and bronze sculptures, and a Grand Canal that is more than 1 mile (1.6 km) long and 200 feet (61 m) wide. Approximately 951,000 gallons (3,600 cu. m) of water are needed to keep the fountains flowing during the weekly "Grande Eaux" water shows. Inside the palace are 2,300 rooms, 2,153 windows, 1,252 fireplaces, and 67 staircases. During the time of Louis XIV, thousands of people lived and worked at Versailles.

Versailles Palace and Grounds

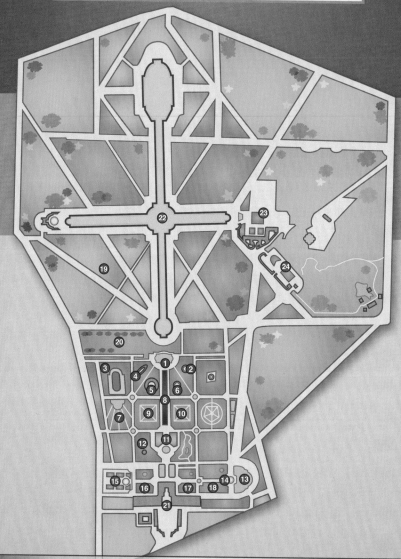

1. Bassin d'Apollon
2. Bosquet de l'Encelade
3. Jardin du Roi
4. Salle des Marronniers
5. Bosquet de la Colonnade
6. Bosquet des Dômes
7. Bassin du Miroir
8. Tapis vert
9. Bosquet de la Girandole
10. Bosquet da Dauphin
11. Bassin et parterre de Latone
12. Salle de Bal
13. Bassin de Neptune
14. Bassin du Dragon
15. Orangerie
16. Parterre Sud
17. Parterre Nord
18. Bosquet de l'Arc de Triomphe
19. Park
20. Gardens
21. Palace
22. Grand Canal
23. Grand Trianon
24. Petit Trianon

Source: PlanetWare, "Versailles Map—Attractions." www.planetware.com.

A Legacy for the Sun King

Louis XIV had one of the longest reigns of any European king, occupying the French throne for seventy-two years. During that time some thirty-six thousand workers labored to build the château in four construction phases. Louis commissioned the best designers and craftsmen to transform his vision into reality. By the time the palace was completed, Versailles featured a chapel, an opera house, and the magnificent Hall of Mirrors, where lavish royal ceremonies took place. The ceremonial aspect of this room continued long after the palace's role as France's seat of power ended: in 1919 the Treaty of Versailles, ending World War I, was signed in the Hall of Mirrors.

The Palace of Versailles has found a place in popular culture. More than 150 films have been photographed at Versailles, dating back as far as 1904. The palace is a natural backdrop for novels, especially those of the romance genre. The fashion industry has found Versailles and its gardens an elegant setting for television commercials. Curators at the palace have teamed with Google to present online virtual exhibitions of Versailles's art treasures and history. Podcasts of Versailles's restoration projects, concerts, and guided tours can be downloaded from Apple's iTunes U. For visitors touring the gardens, a smartphone app provides a three-dimensional map, audio and video commentary, and allows the creation of personal galleries that can be shared on Facebook.

Among the paintings, sculptures, and furniture of Versailles, the image of the sun, usually worked in gold, is prominently displayed throughout the palace. It is the emblem of Apollo, the Greek sun god, that Louis chose as the symbol of his position as *le Roi Soleil*, or "the Sun King." The sun, he wrote in his *Mémoires*, "is surely the most vivid and beautiful image of a monarch."[2] To Louis XIV, the sun was the perfect symbol of his absolute power, and the Palace of Versailles was the perfect setting for his reign as king of France and Navarre.

CHAPTER ONE

The Hunting Lodge

Long before Louis XIV became king, the region where he eventually constructed his magnificent palace was familiar to the monarchs that ruled France before him. The Galie Valley in northern France was a bleak landscape of marshes, creeks, and low hills located about 11 miles (17.7 km) southwest of the center of Paris. The area was so unpleasant that Louis de Rouvroy, duc de Saint-Simon, whose extensive memoirs chronicled as well as criticized the life of Louis XIV, described it as "that most dismal and thankless of spots, without vistas, woods or water, without soil even, for all the surrounding land is quicksand or bog, and the air cannot be healthy."[3] Since the sixteenth century the land had been owned by the Gondis, a wealthy banking family in Florence, Italy.

Nestled in this dreary valley, the sleepy village of Versailles was, in the early seventeenth century, a small farming community of a few hundred inhabitants. The town already had a long history: the first mention of Versailles in historical records dates back to the year 1038. The name *Versailles* likely comes from the Latin word *versare*, meaning "to turn" (as farmers turn the soil to plant their crops), combined with the French *semailles*, denoting cultivation of the land. By the thirteenth century Versailles had become a prosperous town due to its location on the main road between Paris and the bustling coastal region of Normandy. Farmers on their way to deliver their crops and cattle to the ports of Normandy passed through Versailles, often spending a night at one of the town's three inns. Four fairs were held each year, allowing local farmers and merchants to buy from and sell to passing travelers. The fourteenth century, however, brought both wars and the Black Death to Europe, and the little village found itself, like much of the continent, devastated. Versailles slowly recovered over the next centuries, but it never regained its former prosperity. By the early 1600s the village consisted of a small church, the old inns, a run-down château, and a forlorn windmill sitting atop a hill. But what the poor village lacked, the surrounding countryside provided with abundance: plentiful game for the royal passion of hunting.

Since the Middle Ages, hunting had been the sport of kings and nobles, especially in France. Royal hunting parties rode with horses and hounds through the forests surrounding Versailles in the pursuit of wolves, foxes, rabbits, wild boars, and especially stags, or large male deer. King Louis XIII was introduced early to this royal pastime. He first accompanied his father on a hunting trip in 1607, when he was only six years old. They went hawking, using the predatory bird to catch small game and other birds. According to French historian Jacques Levron, during his afternoon outing Louis caught a "levret [a young hare], five or six quail and two partridges."[4] As he grew up he became an avid huntsman and

continued the sport throughout his reign. When a day's hunt ended too late for him to return to the royal residence, Louis XIII and his hunting companions sought shelter wherever they could. The few rough accommodations available in the village were most unsuitable for a king. According to Saint-Simon, Louis "and still more his courtiers, grew tired of sleeping in a low tavern and old windmill, after long, exhausting hunts in the forest of Saint Léger and still further afield."[5] Louis decided that he needed a permanent place near the hunting grounds where he could rest after a long day on the hunt. The old château on the hill might have been converted into such a lodging, but not without a lot of effort. Louis wanted something especially suited for him, so in 1623 the twenty-two-year-old monarch began purchasing land in the Galie Valley, initially acquiring about

French aristocrats embark on a hunt on the grounds of the Palace of Versailles. What began as a relatively simple hunting lodge, blossomed into a grand château—complete with glorious gardens and sumptuous décor.

100 acres (40.5 ha) of the marshy landscape. Next, he commissioned the construction of his own hunting retreat.

Building Louis XIII's Retreat

Imagining a French royal residence usually brings to mind a beautiful palace filled with splendid furnishings and embellished in gold, marble, and precious gems. Indeed, Louis XIV's Versailles would ultimately become the embodiment of royal grandeur. But the foundation of that magnificent structure was his father's humble (from a king's perspective) lodge. Louis XIII selected the hill upon which the old windmill stood as the location for his retreat. This site was later criticized by architect Jacques-François Blondel as "a hillock that rises in the center of a valley surrounded by still higher hills, which gives it a rather diminished appearance."[6] But at the time Louis XIII was not interested in having a lavish showplace at Versailles. All he wanted was somewhere to rest after the hunt and, in addition, to have a place where he could withdraw from the public pressures of being king. A private hunting lodge would fulfill those requirements. In the past Louis XIII had never paid much attention to architecture. Few records exist from the era, but Louis took a personal interest in this project, and it is possible that he designed the lodge himself. For the actual construction he chose Nicolas Huaut, a master mason, to transform his plans into reality.

Work on the lodge began in September 1623. Huaut employed traditional late-medieval construction techniques, building the lodge of rough stone faced with plaster and topping it with a slate roof. Such building materials were not elegant; in fact, they were usually used for lower-class housing. But Louis was satisfied that they would be satisfactory for a part-time residence. Using simple building methods, cheap materials, and a large contingent of laborers, construction went quickly and Louis's hunting lodge was completed in a matter of months. The lodge was a plain two-story structure laid out in a U-shaped design consisting of a main building, or *corps de logis*, with wings extending perpendicularly from each end. The roof of the main section was slightly taller than that of the wings. A wall with a gate at its center connected the ends of the wings, creating an entry courtyard through which guests approached the residence. This courtyard would eventually become the Cour Marbre (Marble Court) of the completed Versailles palace. Surrounding the lodge was a moat about 30 feet (9 m) deep. This was a reminder of medieval cas-

HUNTING WITH THE KING

The history of hunting dates back to ancient times, when it was a vital means of survival for early humans. As the domestication of animals and agriculture began to provide more of humankind's dietary requirements, hunting eventually evolved from an essential activity to a sport. By the seventeenth century hunting was the main form of recreation for the kings and nobles of France. This royal sport was so popular that it had serious consequences for the local ecology. Historian Jean-Marie Pérouse de Montclos explains the perils of this sport of kings:

> In fact, the passion for the hunt, which remained a constant from the first Valois to the last of the Bourbon dynasty [1328 to 1792], placed the local wildlife in great ecological peril. Whether flying fowl or earthbound game, it was relentlessly pursued with firearms, every day and in every season. Whereas Louis XIV contented himself with a daily quota of a single stag, Louis XV required three, increasing the numbers of his horse and hound proportionately. To facilitate replenishment of the natural population through reproduction in the mating season, periodically the hunting parties moved elsewhere. . . . Nonetheless, by the end of the reign of Louis XIV the population of wolves in the Versailles region had been completely wiped out.

Jean-Marie Pérouse de Montclos, *Versailles*. New York: Abbeville, 1991, p. 28.

tles, where water-filled moats provided protection for the castle's inhabitants. The moat surrounding the hunting lodge remained dry due to the difficulty of transporting water up the hill, but it still afforded a measure of security for the king and his entourage. Within the moat, the land upon which the lodge sat was formed into a bastion: a star-shaped fortification commonly found protecting medieval castles.

In front of the lodge was a large outer courtyard flanked by stables on one side and storerooms and lodgings for the stable hands on the other. Louis XIII apparently conceived the idea of and designed the layout for this courtyard. According to an account written by his doctor, Jean Héroard, Louis "went to Mass, fed deer meat to his dogs, came back to the residence, had his musketeers [soldiers] exercise, then decided on the lay out of the courtyard for his house at Versailles."[7] Finally, a wall was constructed surrounding the entire estate to provide privacy and security.

The lodge was a square measuring 115 feet (35 m) on each side. It contained around twenty rooms, with the king's residence apartment located in the central *corps de logis*. In European architecture the lowest level in a building (aside from the basement) is called the ground floor. In French royal residences the first floor, which in the United States would be called the second floor, was often referred to as the noble floor, for it was here that the monarch's accommodations were usually located. Thus, on the first floor of the lodge was the royal apartment that served as the king's living quarters. This apartment comprised four rooms: the king's bedroom, a dressing room, a closet (which today would be called a study or office), and a reception room for greeting visiting dignitaries. Although little additional information remains about the rooms in the lodge, inventories of their furnishings allow a glimpse of the simple style that Louis XIII required while staying there. Although beautiful wall tapestries lent a certain elegance to the apartment, the accommodations were mostly unpretentious. As French historian Levron writes,

The furniture was extremely simple. The bed of green damask had three fustian mattresses, with curtains to match the damask. . . . In the closet were a locked chest, upholstered in leather, two trunks, a table on which were two silver candlesticks with large candles and a writing desk in Eastern leather.

The hunting lodge built by Louis XIII consisted of a U-shaped structure. The central courtyard formed an entryway for guests; it eventually became the completed palace's Marble Court (pictured).

. . . The main ornament of [the closet] was a brand new billiard table with its cover, twelve balls, six cues, and two four-pillared tables. . . . In the King's dressing-room were the inevitable commode, a cupboard in which were hidden the green velvet dressing table and another table covered with green taffetas.[8]

The remaining rooms of the lodge were devoted to various support functions that served the king and kept the household running while he was there. Several rooms in the main building housed the Captains of the Guard, the heads of the king's security force, and other royal attendants. In the wings were apartments for the king's hunting companions as well as storage rooms, latrines, and rooms for Louis XIII's servants, kitchen staff, and soldiers who waited on, cooked for, and provided protection for the king and his followers. An important member of the staff was the concierge, who, with his wife (the only woman allowed to live in the lodge), had a room in one of the wings. Residing year-round at the lodge, the concierge was in charge of maintaining the furniture, a valued job in the king's household. Soon after construction was completed, on March 9, 1624, Louis XIII stayed at his new lodge for the first time.

Along with the lodge, Louis wanted gardens to enhance the natural beauty of his property. Jacques Boyceau, a landscape architect and Louis's superintendent of royal gardens, and Boyceau's nephew Jacques de Menours, designed formal gardens for the lodge that included decorative flowerbeds, water basins, and groves of trees. It was the beginning of the extensive gardens that would bring natural beauty for the enjoyment of generations of visitors to Versailles.

One aspect of the hunting lodge that provides an insight into the character of Louis XIII is the fact that there were no rooms especially reserved for women. When at the lodge, Louis preferred the company of his male companions, and he was irritated by the presence of giggling, primping females. Not even his wife, Queen Anne of Austria, stayed overnight at the lodge. In a letter to his chief minister, Cardinal Richelieu, Louis wrote, "I suppose that the queen could be lodged at Versailles with my children, but I fear her numerous entourage, whose presence here would spoil everything for me."[9] The king did, however, relax his rule of excluding women from the lodge on the occasion of November 1626. Louis invited Queen Anne and his mother, Marie de Médicis, to the retreat, where they shared supper with the king. It was the only time the two women visited the lodge together, and they left before nightfall. Anne would eventually make one more sojourn to Louis's isolated retreat. But this visit would bring her not to the old rustic lodge but to a new and more elegant country estate.

WORDS IN CONTEXT
colonnade
A series of columns joined at the top.

⬡ PALACES BEFORE VERSAILLES

Louis XIV will always be associated with the Palace of Versailles. But before Versailles was built, the court of the French kings was itinerant, moving from one palace to another whenever the king pleased.

St. Germain-en-Laye, where Louis XIV was born, originated as a twelfth-century castle about 12 miles (19.3 km) west of Paris. After centuries of renovation, the palace became the home of King Henry II and later Louis XIII. The palace's gardens were among the first Italian-style gardens created in France, eventually leading to the development of the French formal garden.

Fontainebleau, another royal residence, was continuously occupied by French royalty for some eight hundred years. Located 34 miles (55 km) from Paris, it was the residence of thirty-four monarchs, from Louis VII in 1137 to the end of the Second Empire in 1870. Louis XIII was born there and learned the joys of hunting from his father, King Henry IV.

Like Versailles, the Château of Vincennes began as a twelfth-century hunting lodge. Built in the Vincennes forest, located 4.2 miles (6.8 km) east of Paris, it grew into a true castle featuring a 180-foot-tall (55 m) donjon, or fortified tower, and an outer wall that was 3,937 feet (1,200 m) long. After Henry IV was assassinated in 1610, his wife and son, the heir to the throne, sought refuge at Vincennes.

With Louis XIV's decision to make Versailles the permanent seat of power, the itinerant government of France finally found a home worthy of the king.

A New Château

For years Louis XIII spent many pleasant hours at the hunting lodge. But by 1631 he began to feel that his little hunting lodge, with its rough and low-quality materials, was no longer appropriate for the king of France. With the able assistance of Cardinal Richelieu, Louis had strengthened his royal position by subduing the rebellious Huguenots (French Protestants), bringing headstrong nobles in line, and building a navy. The time seemed right for him to convert the modest hunting lodge into a stylish country manor, or château, more appropriate for a monarch.

Louis's first task was to choose someone to design his château. The one name that stood out was that of Philibert Le Roy. An architect and engineer, Le Roy had been appointed the king's royal architect in 1627. He immediately began working on the design for the new château. Once the king approved Le Roy's plan, construction began in 1631. The old hunting lodge was demolished in stages so that areas not under construction could still be used by the king and his retinue. The *corps de logis* was widened, and the height of the two wings was increased so that all three parts of the building had the same elevation. The wings were extended and at each corner of the lodge a pavilion, or tower, was built. The gated entry wall was torn down and replaced with a colonnade of arches that connected the ends of the wings.

Unlike the rough facade of the original lodge, Louis's new château was constructed of cream-colored stone and red brick. To enhance the decorative effect, the bricks were enriched with red and white paint. The roof was covered in dark blue slate tiles. This striking color scheme was popular in the 1600s. French historian Henri Sauval comments that it "created a variously colored effect so agreeable to contemporaries that it was used for all the great palaces."[10] Completed in 1634, Louis's new country house was an elegant château, far exceeding in design and elegance the little hunting lodge as a place for the king to stay. Still, some of his contemporaries were less than impressed by the château. When the ever-critical Saint-Simon called it a "little card castle"[11] (other translations of his statement are "pasteboard house" and "little house of cards"), he was either comparing it to the inherent instability of a playing-card house or perhaps remarking that the stone and brick exterior resembled the back of such cards.

In the seventeenth century the king of France had several royal residences from which he ruled and lived. Louis XIII spent time at the Louvre palace in Paris, the traditional seat of government, and at the château of St. Germain-en-Laye, located only a few miles from

Formal gardens enhanced the natural beauty of the property. Over time, the gardens (pictured in this engraving) included a vast selection of decorative flower beds, water basins, fountains, and tree groves.

his new château at Versailles. But Versailles was simply a part-time house for Louis's leisure and refreshment, and he conducted no affairs of state while staying there. The king and his companions relaxed by playing billiards and such board games as chess and backgammon. Hunting, of course, was still the primary sport of the king, and he spent an increasing amount of time in the woods around Versailles, retreating to the château at the end of his excursions.

While the construction of the new château was proceeding, Louis XIII acquired more of the surrounding countryside. Jean-François de Gondi, from whom Louis had bought the original tract of land for the hunting lodge, was the archbishop of Paris and the seigneur of Versailles. Dating from the feudalism of the Middle Ages, the seigneurial system framed the relationship between the seigneur and his tenants, who were mostly peasant farmers. Parcels of land were rented to the farmers; they worked the land and paid taxes to the lord or gave him a portion of their harvest. A seigneury, or the legal right to own the land, could be bought and sold at the discretion of the seigneur. In April 1632 Louis XIII purchased the seigneury of Versailles from de Gondi for 60,000 livres. With this acquisition, the extent of his land-holdings more than doubled to around 250 acres (101.2 ha). There was now enough space to extend and enhance the château's gardens.

The Birth of a Dauphin

On November 25, 1615, Louis XIII had married Anne of Austria when they were both just fourteen years old. Anne was the daughter of King Philip III of Spain (her title refers to the fact that Spanish kings were of the royal House of Austria—also known as the Haps-burgs). Their marriage was an arranged union, formed to strengthen the political and military alliance between France and Spain. From the outset, Louis XIII's attitude toward his queen was one of distance and indifference. Although she was the wife of the French monarch, Anne irritated Louis by continuing to dress and act as if she were still in her Spanish homeland. This was seen by many as arrogance and an affront to the king. Efforts to bring them closer together by Charles d'Albert, duc de Luynes, a member of Louis's court, met with some success. But Anne suffered a series of miscarriages between 1619 and 1631, and Louis once more spurned his queen. For the next seven years it seemed that Anne might never produce a legacy for Louis and an heir to the throne of France.

On September 5, 1638, Louis's prayers were answered when a long-awaited son was born. "We have a Dauphin!"[12] said Louis, using the term for a king's eldest son, the next in line to the French throne. Many regarded the birth of the future Sun King as a miracle. He was born on Sunday (the day of the sun), and it was naively said that the sun was especially close to the earth on that morning. Madame de Motteville, a servant of the queen, remarked in her memoirs that the newborn dauphin was a "child-King, like a gift given by Heaven in answer to their [the French peoples'] prayers."[13]

The young Louis was a robust child, unlike his father who had endured a lifetime of poor health and suffered from tuberculosis and intestinal problems. "Louis XIII trailed his shattered health about with him all his life," writes French historian Victor Lucien Tapié, "his most frequent ailments being attacks of enteritis which left him exhausted in body and dejected in spirit."[14] By the spring of 1643 Louis XIII's health had deteriorated so much that he began to get his affairs in order, including arrangements for the baptism of his son, which took place on April 21. On May 14, 1643, King Louis XIII died in his bed of ulcerative colitis, surrounded by members of his court. At his passing his son received the title of king of France. He was four years and eight months old.

Among the new dauphin's inheritance was his father's château in the village of Versailles. But it would remain empty for the next twenty years as young Louis prepared to take his place as the absolute monarch of France.

CHAPTER TWO

Building the Palace of Versailles

The early years of Louis XIV's life bore several similarities to those of his father, Louis XIII. Both assumed the mantle of king as a child upon the death of their fathers. (Henry IV, Louis XIII's father and the first king of the House of Bourbon, had been assassinated on May 14, 1610, thirty-three years to the day before the death of his son.) As both were in their minority (not yet of legal age) their mothers acted as regent, or temporary head of state. Aided by experienced chief ministers, Marie de Médicis and Anne of Austria ruled France in their sons' stead. Both Louis XIII and Louis XIV wed Spanish infantas (daughters of royalty) in marriages arranged for political purposes.

Anne's chief minister was Cardinal Jules Mazarin, who had served under Louis XIII until the king's death in 1643. Born in Italy but becoming a French citizen in 1639, Mazarin was godfather to the young monarch. He was instrumental in negotiating treaties that put France in a strong political position in Europe. One of his most important jobs was supervising Louis's education. Under his guidance, Louis learned mathematics, history, geography, dancing, Italian and Latin, and drawing. Mazarin also made sure that Louis learned about politics, with all of its intrigue, plots, and alliances. But most of all, Mazarin instilled in Louis the love of grandeur and the glory of the monarchy.

Louis was a healthy and handsome child, taking after his grand-father, Henry IV, rather than his distant and sickly father. Madame de Motteville, Anne's lady-in-waiting, describes a young Louis at a dance:

> His fine features, his sweet, yet serious, expression, the pink and white of his complexion, and his hair, which was at that time very fair and curly, became him far better than his clothes. He danced perfectly, and . . . he was one of the most distinguished and certainly the most handsome of those pres-ent, although he was only eight years old.[15]

Along with his love of music and dancing, Louis was fascinated with military affairs, an attraction that stayed with him for the rest of his life. He enjoyed playing with toy soldiers and participating in war games with his friends on the grounds of the Louvre. His attraction to arms and combat, however, was not limited to play. Wars were a constant part of life in seventeenth-century Europe, and Louis would review his troops on horseback, dressed in full royal regalia. While Louis enjoyed playing military games and seeing his real troops off to war, a civil uprising within his own country had a profoundly different effect on the young king.

The Frondes

During the years when Louis was growing from childhood, through adolescence, to young adulthood, France was undergoing funda-mental changes. Since the fifteenth century the nation had existed under the social and political system known as the *ancien régime*, or "old order." French society was divided into three classes: nobles, or rich landowners; middle-class craftsmen and merchants known as the bourgeoisie; and peasant farmers, who toiled on the nobles' land and made up the vast majority of the population. The nobles not only had wealth, they also had political power. The *parlements*, or supreme courts, were largely made up of the nobility. They played a large role in

Louis XIV often wore full royal regalia while reviewing his troops on horseback. A seventeenth-century portrait captures the spirit and showmanship of the French king.

influencing, and often obstructing, the judicial decisions made by the king or his chief minister.

As Cardinal Richelieu worked to strengthen Louis XIII's monarchy, the nobles began to lose some of their influence. This decline continued under Louis XIV's chief minister, Cardinal Mazarin. Already burdened with rising taxes to fund ongoing wars, the nobility became alarmed at their diminishing political power and decided to do something about it. Between 1648 and 1653, two rebellions called

Frondes (named after a child's slingshot) rocked the nation. The city's *parlement* began a protest against new taxes, and soon sympathetic mobs rioted in the streets of Paris. "The mob has taken up arms," wrote Queen Anne. "Barricades have been put up in the streets. . . .

The evil may grow to a point where the royal authority may be destroyed."[16] Protesters hurled insults at Queen Anne, who was so terrified that she, along with young King Louis and Cardinal Mazarin, fled the city.

Eventually Parisians grew tired of the bloodshed of the Frondes and peace returned to France in 1653. The fifteen-year-old king returned to Paris and was cheered by the populace. But he never forgot the rebellion and the fear that it instilled in him. He would never again trust the nobles to remain loyal to him or to the throne.

Return to Versailles

The years 1660 and 1661 saw important milestones in the life of Louis XIV. Political expediency demanded that Louis, like his father, marry a Spanish infanta. The arranged marriage of Louis to Marie-Thérèse, daughter of King Philip IV of Spain, took place on June 9, 1660. His marriage, however, did not prevent Louis from having affairs with numerous mistresses. One such courtesan, Louise de La Vallière, caught Louis's eye, and they regularly left Paris to spend time in the seclusion of Versailles. "We often went to Versailles," she wrote. "No one was allowed to follow the King there without his order."[17] Some say that Louis fell in love with Madame de La Vallière and Versailles at the same time.

On March 9, 1661, Cardinal Mazarin died. Upon his passing, Louis, who was now twenty-two years old, lost a beloved godfather and an invaluable teacher and adviser. Speculation in France now centered on whom Louis would choose to take Mazarin's place. But Louis stunned the nation by making a historic decision: he would rule France without the counsel of a chief minister. The day after Mazarin's death, Louis held a meeting of his advisers and said, "I have summoned you with my Ministers and Secretaries of State to tell you that until now I have been quite willing to let my affairs be managed by the Cardinal; in future I shall be my own Prime Minister."[18] Louis's rule as absolute monarch had begun.

One of Louis's first tasks was deciding what to do with his devious finance minister, Nicolas Fouquet. Appointed to the post of *surintendant des finances* by Cardinal Mazarin, Fouquet was a man of great ambition but little integrity. Fouquet controlled the treasury

---

⬡ A GREAT MORTALITY

Construction work is inherently dangerous, and this was no less true for the thousands of men who labored to build Versailles and its gardens. By 1685 about thirty-six thousand men, many of them royal soldiers, were performing construction work at Versailles. Working from wooden scaffoldings, many workers died in falls, and others were run over by horse-drawn carts carrying construction materials or removing dirt from the excavations. Leveling the swampy ground for the gardens was a dirty and dangerous task that reportedly took many lives as workers were buried under fallen embankments. Disease took its toll as well, as insect-borne diseases felled other workers.

Marie de Rabutin-Chantal, marquise de Sévigné, who penned numerous letters on life at Versailles, wrote of the hazards of construction in 1678:

> The King wishes to go to Versailles on Saturday, but God, it seems, wills otherwise, because of the impossibility of getting the buildings in a fit state to receive him, and because of the great mortality afflicting the workmen, of whom every night wagons full of the dead are carried out as though from the Hotel-Dieu [hospital]. These melancholy processions are kept secret as far as possible, in order not to alarm the other workmen.

Quoted in Gilette Ziegler, *At the Court of Versailles: Eye-Witness Reports from the Reign of Louis XIV*. New York: Dutton, 1966, p. 30.

of France, negotiating with lenders and deciding where the government's money should go. The fact that a good deal of that money went into his own secret accounts would be his downfall. Fouquet was unaware that Louis had evidence of his misconduct. On August 17, 1661, he boldly held a splendid fete, or celebration, to honor the king and to flaunt his newly completed château, Vaux-le-Vicomte. The château was a masterwork of seventeenth-century architecture. Six thousand guests were awed by its exquisite tapestries and Persian carpets, gilded mirrors, and crystal chandeliers. Fouquet's fatal mistake was outshining the king with this lavish display of wealth. Several weeks later Fouquet was arrested and, following a three-year trial, was sentenced to life in prison, where he died in 1680.

Fouquet had left in disgrace, but Louis could not keep Vaux-le-Vicomte from his thoughts. Surely the king deserved a château just as magnificent as his former finance minister's. In Vaux-le-Vicomte, Louis envisioned what Versailles could become. And he was determined to turn that vision into reality.

Planning Versailles

Not everyone was convinced that Versailles was the best location for a royal palace. Jean-Baptiste Colbert, who succeeded Fouquet as finance minister, was also France's minister of buildings. In a letter to the king, he lamented Louis's choice of location for his palace:

> Your majesty knows that apart from brilliant actions in war nothing marks better the grandeur and genius of princes than their buildings, and that posterity measures them by the standard of the superb edifices which they erect during their lives. Oh, what a pity that the greatest king and the most virtuous, should be measured by the standard of Versailles![19]

The marriage of Louis XIV of France and Marie-Thérèse, the daughter of the Spanish king, is celebrated in 1660. Their union reinforced the reconciliation between France and Spain.

But Louis would not be dissuaded, and he ordered Colbert to find the money to build the palace. While the finance minister began examining the accounts, Louis pondered who would be the best men to transform his father's château into the most magnificent structure in the world. Once again, he needed to look no further than Vaux-le-Vicomte. Three men were responsible for the design of Fouquet's magnificent palace: architect Louis Le Vau, landscape designer André Le Nôtre, and artist Charles Le Brun. Le Vau had held the post of chief architect to the king since 1654, working on the Louvre and the Tuileries, the royal residences in Paris. Le Nôtre was the king's personal gardener, who had become rich designing French formal gardens. Le Brun, a master of seventeenth-century French art, had begun receiving art commissions from wealthy patrons at age fifteen. Louis considered him the greatest French artist of all time. Taken alone, each man was the best in his field; as a team, their talents combined to create Fouquet's grand palace. Louis knew that they could create for him an even greater masterpiece at Versailles.

There was, however, still the problem of funding for the new palace. Much of France's wealth was being spent in pursuing wars fought with the goal of expanding the nation's empire. In 1659 France and Spain signed the Treaty of the Pyrenees, ending a ten-year conflict between the two nations. Money became available for other purposes, including Versailles. Construction on the palace took place in four campaigns over a fifty-year period, from around 1661 to 1710. The start of each building campaign coincided with a peace treaty being signed between France and the nation it was fighting. The money that had been financing the wars was funneled into construction work on Versailles.

The First Campaign

The initial building campaign was modest compared to those that would follow. The French royal treasury was still low on funds after the war, so work had to be done slowly until the coffers were once more built up by taxes. While few records exist to document the work that went on in the first phase of construction, several changes in the château are known to have taken place at this time. Louis XIII's château originally had been built without hallways; the interior *enfilade* chambers occupied the full width of the structure. Thus the only way to move through the château was to go through the rooms themselves. A balcony with an iron railing was constructed around the entire first floor, making movement from room to room easier. The buildings bordering the outer courtyard (now called the Cour Royale, or Royal Court) that served as stables and storerooms were rebuilt and enlarged, their design following the stone and brick motif of the main building.

Changes to the interior arrangement of the château were influenced by Louis's view on women. Unlike his father, Louis did not prohibit a female presence in the château. Both his mother, Anne of Austria, and his wife, Marie-Thérèse, were welcome at Versailles. An apartment was made for Anne on the ground floor, and Marie had living quarters on the first floor, opposite the king's apartment. The interior of Versailles was lavishly decorated with paintings, tapestries, and sculptures, many of which had been confiscated from Vaux-le-Vicomte after the fall of Fouquet.

As Louis grew in confidence and stature, his plans for Versailles expanded as well. The next building campaign would begin the remarkable transformation of the hunting lodge to a magnificent showplace.

The Second Campaign

According to Colbert, the hunting lodge was too small and too ordinary for a king of Louis's stature. He felt that it should be demolished to make way for a new building. In a memo to the king, Colbert stated, "There are, then, two options to consider: preservation of that which is extant, with worthless results; or destruction of this, with a new, small structure to be in its place."[20] But Louis was adamant that the lodge be spared, declaring that if it were torn down, he would simply have it rebuilt.

So the lodge, by this time aging and in need of repair, had to remain. Le Vau's solution to the problem of keeping the lodge while creating a new grand palace for the king was an ingenious plan called the envelope. In October 1668 workers began building a new U-shaped structure around the perimeter of the lodge, thus "enveloping" it while keeping the old building intact. The eastern side, the open end of the "U," which remained as an entry court, received marble paving, giving it the name Marble Court. Le Vau designed the interior side of the envelope in stone and brick to harmonize with the exterior design of the lodge, and the outer walls were constructed of stone in a more modern Italian style. The construction formed two new interior courtyards on the north and south sides of the lodge.

As Louis saw the new walls rising around the old lodge, he began

> **WORDS IN CONTEXT**
> enfilade
> *A series of connected rooms having doorways aligned with each other.*

to have misgivings. Perhaps, he thought, Colbert was right and the old lodge should be demolished after all. The king arranged a competition among six architects to see if a better plan for the palace could be devised. But none of the architects could come up with a suitable proposal, and work on the envelope continued.

The exterior facade of the envelope featured arched windows on the ground floor, and the walls were accented with horizontal grooves to emphasize the massive strength of the stonework. The first floor had square windows separated by pilasters. The roof was low-pitched so that it was barely visible from ground level, and a third floor, or attic, was constructed. In the interior of the palace, the king's apartment was expanded, with a series of enfilade rooms constructed in the northern wing of the envelope. This was the king's Grand Apartment, an addition to the smaller and more private, interior apartment located in the original structure. The Grand Apartment was where the king conducted the public business of the government. Entrance to the Grand Apartment was by way of the Ambassador's Staircase, a grand red marble stairway that was used by Louis XIV, although ultimately demolished by his successor. The queen's apartment, a suite of five rooms, was located opposite the king's in the southern wing. In the western, or garden, side of the palace a long, open terrace separated the two royal apartments.

The Third Campaign

On October 11, 1670, Louis Le Vau died in Paris. His assistant, François d'Orbay, continued Le Vau's work until 1675, when Louis appointed Jules Hardouin Mansart as chief architect. Mansart's most important addition to Versailles was the Grande Galerie, now best known as the Galerie des Glaces, or the Hall of Mirrors. Beginning construction in 1678, he appropriated two rooms from the king's and queen's apartments, which became the Salon of War and the Salon of Peace. Between these rooms was Le Vau's open terrace, which Mansart now enclosed with a wall connecting to the rest of the western facade. On this side of the hall Mansart placed seventeen arched

The Palace of Versailles construction site, as it looked around 1680 during the Third Campaign, shows significant progress. By 1682 Louis had officially moved the seat of French government to Versailles.

windows to provide a magnificent view of the gardens beyond. On the opposite wall, seventeen mirrored arches reflected the light that streamed from the windows. Each arch contained 21 mirrors, for a grand total of 357. Between the mirrors were marble pilasters topped with gilded capitals. Measuring 239.5 feet (73 m) long and 34.4 feet (10.5 m) wide, the Hall of Mirrors included forty-three chandeliers that held one thousand candles to illuminate the hall at night.

The breathtaking magnificence of the Hall of Mirrors confirmed Louis's status as the absolute monarch of France. "The grand gallery," writes historian James Eugene Farmer, "is the epitome of absolutism and divine right and the grandeur of the House of Bourbon."[21] In 1682 Louis officially moved the seat of French government to

Versailles, turning his back on Paris and confirming the palace as a symbol of his royal power. As large as the palace was, more space was needed for the growing number of occupants. Mansart designed two massive buildings—the Northern and Southern Wings—to be constructed on a north-south axis extending from the buildings on either side of the Royal Court. Construction of the Southern Wing had begun in 1678 and was completed in 1682. Three years later work began on the Northern Wing, but in 1689 construction was halted as money was needed for yet another war.

Because of this war, construction also stopped on another of Mansart's designs: the new Royal Chapel. It would be ten years before workmen returned to complete the structure.

The Fourth Campaign

When the war ended in 1699, the construction of the Royal Chapel resumed. Building the chapel became the only project of the Fourth Campaign. Mansart's design included such characteristic Gothic elements as gargoyles and flying buttresses in addition to classical Corinthian columns. Built at the south end of the Northern Wing, the two-story chapel's high-pitched roof soars above the rest of the palace, emphasizing Louis XIV's devotion to the Catholic Church. Large windows allow abundant light to enter the chapel, but unlike traditional Gothic windows, they feature clear rather than stained glass. The interior walls were finished in stone rather than more elegant marble for fear that marble would create a damp environment for the king's worship.

WORDS IN CONTEXT

pilaster
An ornamental flattened column, with or without fluting, including a base and capital and attached to a wall as decoration.

After Mansart's death in 1708, his associate Robert de Cotte took over the project, which was completed in 1710. Louis, seventy-two years old at the time, regularly attended daily Mass and other services there. On August 15, 1715, he attended the Feast of Saint

◆ ROYAL REFLECTIONS

Mirrors are so commonplace today that most people never give them a second thought. But in the seventeenth century they were a rare and expensive luxury. Almost all mirrors of the time were manufactured in Venice, Italy, creating a virtual monopoly of the industry. Louis XIV wanted to have mirrors in his palace, as much for a display of status as for his own vanity. But his finance minister, Colbert, balked at the exorbitant cost of Venetian mirrors. In 1665 Colbert established a company called the Manufacture Royale de Glaces de Miroirs, or Royal Manufactory of Mirrors, to supply Versailles, as well as other palaces and government buildings, with mirrors. He secretly brought in glassworkers from Venice to create the mirrors as well as to train French craftsmen in the art. But some say that Italian agents entered France and poisoned Colbert's Venetian workers in an effort to preserve the nation's monopoly.

Manufacturing mirrors was a difficult and dangerous process that involved coating panes of glass with a reflective layer of mercury, a highly toxic chemical. Many workers in the industry died from mercury poisoning. Eventually the manufactory was able to produce mirrors that surpassed Venetian mirrors in size and quality. In 1678 it began its greatest challenge: making the 357 mirrors for Versailles's Hall of Mirrors.

By the turn of the eighteenth century, mirrors had become an essential element of French Baroque architecture, with Versailles as a leading example of the glassmakers' art.

Louis; it was the last time Louis would visit the chapel. He was suffering from gangrene of the leg, a condition that could not be cured by the medicine of the time. Louis spent the last week of his life in bed, putting his affairs in order. Versailles had been Louis's crown jewel, but according to art historian Pierre Verlet, he "loved architecture to the point where he reproached himself on his deathbed for having loved buildings too much."[22] Death came to the Sun King on September 1, 1715, just four days short of his seventy-seventh birthday. He had ruled France for seventy-two years, longer than any European monarch before or since.

With the king's passing, the fourth and last major building campaign came to a close. Versailles was a magnificent legacy for Louis XIV, but it was still incomplete. Louis XV, the Sun King's great-grandson and successor, oversaw the construction of a grand theater at the opposite end of the Northern Wing from where the chapel stood. Plans for the Royal Opera were drawn in 1765 by architect Ange-Jacques Gabriel, working from a design originally conceived by Mansart. Construction began the same year and was completed in 1770. Although the interior appears to be marble, the walls are actually wood painted with a faux marble design. The Royal Opera was an example of the best in theater design of its day; with seating for more than seven hundred attendees, it was the largest theater in Europe. Its unique oval plan allowed for unrestricted sight lines and superior acoustics from any seat. Louis XV often enjoyed lavish performances in the Royal Opera, preferring to view the productions from a screened private box that hid his face from the crowd.

The Palace of Versailles is a splendid example of seventeenth-century French Baroque architecture. But it is only part of the grandeur that is Versailles. Surrounding the palace is a vast panorama of gardens that are a testament to the genius of André Le Nôtre, the landscape architect who designed them.

CHAPTER THREE

The Gardens of Versailles

I f the gardens of Versailles, French writer Jean Cocteau recalled, "There was a swamp. And there were architects and gardeners. And there were lines, angles, triangles, rectangles, circles, and pyramids. And there was a park, and this park was born of the soul of Le Nôtre."[23] André Le Nôtre had gardening not only in his soul but in his family as well. His grandfather and father were both landscape designers whose work included the gardens of the Tuileries in Paris. Le Nôtre learned about gardening from his father, but his education did not end there. He studied art under artist Simon Vouet, court painter to Louis XIII, learning about perspective, optics, and geometry. He also studied architecture and mathematics at the Louvre's academy of arts, where he met Charles Le Brun, the artist with whom he and Louis Le Vau would work at Vaux-le-Vicomte and Versailles.

At Vaux-le-Vicomte, Le Nôtre created a new standard for French formal gardens. He built on the ideas of Italian gardeners, whose plans transformed the typical garden of the time into a pleasing retreat rather than merely a supplier of provisions for the kitchen. Le Nôtre's gardens featured parterres—flat garden beds divided by hedges forming geometric designs—as well as gravel walkways, grottoes, statuary, water basins, and fountains that played with the element of moving water interacting with sunlight. Le Nôtre's work at Vaux-le-Vicomte was revolutionary in its scope. "Up until the design of Vaux-le-Vicomte," comments garden historian Frédéric Sichet, "landscapers were doing less ambitious work. Vaux-le-Vicomte was the first time that a landscape designer oversaw the entire project—the gardens, the fountains, the water, everything. Le Nôtre was given carte blanche. And what he did was a real rupture with what had been done before."[24]

Le Nôtre's genius was unmistakable at Vaux-le-Vicomte. But his greatest work was yet to come at the palace of Louis XIV.

Versailles

Jacques Boyceau and Jacques de Menours were the first landscapers commissioned to design the formal garden for the lodge. Located just west of the palace, the geometric design was called a *parterre de broderie*, or embroidered terrace, which used plantings laid out in graceful, flowing forms resembling embroidered cloth. Ground cover of crushed brick, gravel, or porcelain provided a colorful background to the foliage. Walkways allowed visitors to enjoy leisurely strolls around the garden. A central path was arranged on an east-west line beginning at the west facade of the château, creating a geographic axis that formed the backbone around which future expansion would be made. A large pool, called the Rondeau, was located at the end of the central path and denoted the boundary of the formal gardens. This layout was preserved in a drawing known as the Du Bus plan (named for the man who discovered it, Charles Du Bus), which shows the gardens as they looked before Le Nôtre began his work.

> **WORDS IN CONTEXT**
> mattock
> *A digging or chopping tool with a flat blade.*

Le Nôtre's Plan

In 1662, while Le Vau was beginning his work on the palace, Le Nôtre was planning the gardens. The first task he faced was the preparation of the ground where the gardens would be laid out. The uneven and swampy site had to be leveled, drained, and cleared of weeds and other

Louis and his entourage enjoy an afternoon beside the Parterre du Nord. The Versailles gardens featured numerous parterres—flat garden beds divided by hedges that formed geometric designs.

undesirable vegetation. In an era before modern excavation tools such as bulldozers and backhoes existed, this grueling work had to be done by sheer manpower. Thousands of workers used simple hand tools to clear and reshape the land. In his 1709 book, *La Théorie et la pratique du jardinage* (*The Theory and Practice of Gardening*), eighteenth-century gardener and author Antoine-Joseph Dezallier d'Argenville wrote, "When the earth is to be dug or cut to make a terrace, a bank, a bowling-green or a canal, they make use of mattocks, pickaxes, spades and shovels, with workers who remain behind those who dig and fill baskets, scuttles and wheel-barrows."[25]

Le Nôtre familiarized himself with the grounds of Versailles by walking the land; during construction, the king would often accompany his chief landscaper. "He [the king] took great pleasure in gardens," recalled historian Verlet, "was very interested in flowers and

⬡ THE MARLY MACHINE

Water was an important element of the gardens of Versailles, but transporting it to the palace was no easy achievement. Horse-powered pumps, windmills, and reservoirs all proved inadequate for supplying enough water to the increasing number of fountains in the gardens. The Seine River, located about 5 miles (8 km) from Versailles, was the closest source of abundant water. But its banks were well below the level of the palace; some kind of massive machine would be needed to raise the Seine's waters the 532 feet (162 m) needed to carry it to Versailles.

The Marly machine was the solution to the problem. Designed by Arnold De Ville and Rennequin Sualem, the enormous wooden mechanism consisted of fourteen waterwheels straddling the Seine, each approximately 39 feet (12 m) in diameter. The wheels were driven by the flow of the river and fed 221 pumps. Using a series of pumping stations and reservoirs, the pumps brought the water in stages uphill to the level of an aqueduct at Louveciennes, then to the palaces at Marly and Versailles. Completed in 1684, the Marly machine pumped 1.3 million gallons (4.9 million L) of water per day from the Seine. A complicated mechanism that was noisy and tended to break down often, it took sixty full-time workers to keep it running.

Although it was replaced in 1817, the Marly machine was a true engineering marvel at a time when the science of hydraulics was in its infancy.

enjoyed planting rare trees. His personal taste was reflected in the magnificence of Versailles."[26] Using his knowledge of design and geometry and employing simple surveyor's tools, Le Nôtre organized his plan for the gardens around the east-west axis of the existing garden. Although few of Le Nôtre's plans exist, from what is known about practical surveying methods of the era from sources such as Dezallier d'Argenville's book, it is likely that Le Nôtre used stakes and measuring lines or chains to lay out the basic design of the gardens. A level with vials, similar to a modern carpenter's level, helped assure a flat ground, and a tracing staff would have been used to draw the designs on the ground.

Building on Boyceau's original layout, Le Nôtre began with the Jardin Haut, the upper garden close to the palace. There he placed, in a north-south alignment, six parterres with geometric hedges, flowerbeds, and fountains, and two bosquets, or groves of trees. Just beyond the upper garden was the lower garden, the Jardin Bas, where the majority of the garden's bosquets were to be found. Farther west, walkways called allées extended into the Petit Parc, or Small Park. Historian Francis Loring Payne describes the gardens:

> The avenues were of white sand, with grassy by-ways on either side bordered by elms and iron railings six or seven feet [1.8 or 2.1 m] high. Beyond these were thickets and niches where statues, sculptured urns and benches of white carved stone were placed. Occasional archways of green led down dim arbors to new enchantments. Here and there were round or star-shaped retreats whose carpets of grass were sprayed by murmuring fountains. In each recess were marble pedestals, busts, a long bench that invited repose.[27]

Beyond the Petit Parc was the great hunting park. The entire garden was enclosed by walls and bounded by roads leading to nearby villages. Of the many parterres Le Nôtre designed, one was unique. On the south side of the palace, the fragrance of citrus filled the summer air.

The Orangerie

For hundreds of years before the time of Louis XIV, orange trees were prized in Europe for their fragrance and delicious fruit. Originating in southeast Asia thousands of years ago, sweet oranges were introduced to Europe during the fifteenth century by Portuguese traders. Louis was particularly fond of the aromatic delicacy and wanted to include orange trees at Versailles. But the delicate nature of the trees required a mild climate, and French winters would have killed the valuable trees. He left it to architect Le Vau to come up with a solution to the problem. Beneath the south parterre Le Vau built a structure called the Orangerie. Its facade of twelve arches looked out onto a lower parterre in front of the Orangerie. Nearly two hundred orange trees, which Louis had confiscated from Vaux-le-Vicomte, were placed there in the warmer months, usually from May to October. They were arranged in rows surrounding neat lawns and a central basin. The trees were planted in wooden boxes rather than permanently located in the ground. As winter approached, the trees were moved into the Orangerie for protection from winter temperatures using a special wheeled machine designed to transport them.

After Mansart took over as architect of Versailles, he enlarged the Orangerie, creating a central vaulted gallery 509 feet (155 m) long. Twice the size of the original, the new Orangerie was large enough to accommodate some two thousand trees as well as other exotic plants that needed protection from cold weather. Galleries extending from the Orangerie on both sides of the lower parterre were topped by long stairways (the *escaliers des cent marches*, or "stairways of one hundred steps") leading from the south parterre to the Orangerie parterre below.

The Bosquets at Versailles

Whereas parterres provided open spaces in the gardens, the bosquets created shady retreats. According to author Stéphane Pincas, the bosquets served as an exterior continuation of the palace.

The French garden extended the style of the interior of the château out into the open. Parterres were carpets, allées were lined with walls of greenery, and bosquets were arranged as outdoor rooms. . . . Decorated with tables, sideboards, lamp-stands and vases, the gardens of Versailles soon became the best-appointed open-air museum of French statuary of the seventeenth century.[28]

The Jardin Bas had fourteen bosquets, each one featuring a different design. Work on the bosquets began in 1663, with the planting of trees forming the Bosquet of the Waterspout and the Bosquet of the Dauphin. Oak, beech, elm, and other types of mature trees were acquired from all over France, including some taken from Vaux-le-Vicomte, and replanted in the bosquets. Fountains adorned the bosquets, and pathways often arranged in geometric patterns crisscrossed the groves. One in particular, the Labyrinth, was a maze of hedges that became popular with visitors. Charles Perrault, a French author best known for his "Tales of Mother Goose," wrote, "It is a square, young wood, very thick and luxuriant, cut into a great number of paths, intermingled with such artifice that nothing is so easy nor so pleasant than to lose one's way."[29] The Labyrinth included three hundred animal sculptures placed on thirty-nine fountains that represented Aesop's fables. Despite its popularity, the Labyrinth was demolished by order of Louis XVI in 1778 and was replaced by the Bosquet de la Reine (the Queen's Grove).

WORDS IN CONTEXT
domain
A territory over which a ruler exercises authority.

The Royal Menagerie

The forerunner of the modern zoo, known as a menagerie, has been traced as far back as 3500 BCE. During the Middle Ages, heads of state built menageries and collected exotic animals from all over the world for the amusement of the royal families. This often meant pit-

The entrance to the maze of hedges and pathways known as the Labyrinth began with thick, verdant stands of trees (pictured). Inside the Labyrinth stood three hundred animal sculptures.

ting animals against each other in deadly fights, cruel spectacles that lingered well into the seventeenth century. In 1662 Louis XIV ordered Le Vau to design and build a menagerie at Versailles. It was the first structure to be built in the gardens, located nearly 1 mile (1.6 km) from the palace. In Louis's menagerie, the animals would not be forced to fight; instead, they would be displayed for all to see and enjoy. In addition, it would display all the animals in one location rather than caging them in different areas of the royal domain, as was the custom of the time.

Completed in 1664, the Menagerie was a two-story building with a central block of reception rooms and a gallery connecting it to a domed octagonal pavilion. A balcony encircled the upper floor of the octagon, allowing visitors to observe the animals that were exhibited in seven radiating outdoor enclosures. Birds were the first creatures to be displayed at the menagerie, and visitors marveled at the ostriches, egrets, cranes, and Egyptian herons. Eventually lions, camels, an elephant, and a rhinoceros joined the menagerie, along with such mundane animals as horses, cows, ducks, and chickens.

Aside from providing the experience of viewing wild animals, the Menagerie also was a setting for advancement in art and the zoological sciences. Artists were able to study the Menagerie's animals, increasing the accuracy of anatomy in their paintings. Louis engaged Flemish artist Nicasius Bernaerts to paint portraits of all the animals in the Menagerie, hanging the paintings in the connecting gallery and the octagonal pavilion. Scientists studied the more than fifty species of animals in the Menagerie, learning about their anatomy by dissecting the animals that died. At times, Louis himself would observe the dissections.

Water in the Gardens

Whether lying in calm reflecting pools, cascading in the woods, or arching high into the sky from elaborately sculptured fountains, water was both a decorative and a symbolic element at Versailles. The king was eager to fill the gardens with fountains and ponds of pure, clean water, something that was scarce for the ordinary citizen of seventeenth-century France. To Louis, such an extravagance further enhanced his status as the all-powerful Sun King. Indeed, much of

THE GROTTO OF THETIS

One of the most interesting buildings in the gardens was the Grotto of Thetis. Begun in 1664, the grotto was located in the Parterre du Nord just north of the palace. It was a simple single-story building with three arched gates on the front facade. According to Charles Perrault, whose brother, Claude, designed the structure, above the center gate "was a golden Sun that spread its rays, also of gold, over the extent of the three gates. . . . It appeared as though the Sun was in the Grotto, and that one saw it through the bars of the gate."

The interior of the Grotto of Thetis was covered in pebbles and sea shells, a popular decoration known as rocaille. Inside were three alcoves, containing sculptures that were probably the work of Charles Le Brun. The sculpture in the central alcove depicted Apollo resting at the end of the day, being attended by the sea goddess Thetis and several sea nymphs. The two side alcoves contained statues of Apollo's horses and their attendants. Aside from its symbolic purpose, the Grotto of Thetis had a practical function: its roof served as a reservoir that stored water for the garden's numerous fountains.

The grotto's location near the palace ultimately sealed its fate. It was demolished in 1684 to make way for the construction of the Northern Wing of the palace. Fortunately, the marvelous statues were preserved and eventually relocated to the Bosquet of the Baths of Apollo.

Quoted in Ian Thompson, *The Sun King's Garden: Louis XIV, André Le Nôtre, and the Creation of the Gardens of Versailles*. New York: Bloomsbury, 2006, p. 143.

the iconography of the fountains in the gardens makes reference to Apollo, the god of the sun and Louis's chosen symbol.

In Louis XIII's garden, the pool known as the Rondeau denoted the far end of the garden. Between 1668 and 1671 Le Nôtre took that pond and transformed it into the Bassin d'Apollon—the Apollo Basin. The central sculpture of the basin, a fountain called the Chariot of the Sun, was designed by Le Brun and carried out by sculptor

Jean-Baptiste Tuby. Constructed of gold-clad lead alloy, it depicts the god Apollo in his chariot pulled by four horses, rising out of the water. The sculpture represents the sun ascending over the horizon to bring light to a new day (even though the statue faces west, the opposite of sunrise).

Just east of the Apollo Basin, the oval Bassin de Latone, or Latona Basin, continues the Apollo theme. Originally called the Frog Fountain for its water-spouting frog sculptures, in 1668 Louis ordered it dedicated to the myth of Latona, the mother of Apollo. Central to the fountain is a marble sculpture of Latona and her twin children, Apollo and Diana. Mansart created a four-tiered marble base with the sculpture at the top. The fountain conveys the elements of the myth: after selfish peasants refuse to give Latona water from a pond for her thirsty children, she calls down a curse that turns the peasants into frogs, who must forever live in the pond. Below the Latona sculpture are figures of peasants transforming into frogs as well as animals such as frogs, lizards, and turtles. The fountain symbolizes the protection that God bestowed upon Apollo and his family. Some historians interpret the fountain as a representation of Louis XIV's victory over the Frondes.

WORDS IN CONTEXT
radiating
Extending from a central point.

The largest and most impressive body of water at Versailles is the Grand Canal. Following the line of the east-west axis, the Grand Canal is 1 mile (1.6 km) long and 203.4 feet (62 m) wide. It is crossed midway by a slightly shorter transverse canal, the south end of which terminates near the Menagerie. Construction of the Grand Canal began in 1668 with the formidable task of excavating the marshy ground; it took eleven years to complete. Rows of majestic oak, ash, and other species of trees lined the 3.4 mile (5.5 km) perimeter of the canal. Along with its decorative function, the Grand Canal played a practical role at Versailles. Situated at the lowest point in the gardens, the canal collected water from the numerous fountains for repumping along miles of underground pipes. It also provided a scenic water route for gondolas to take guests to the Menagerie at the southern tip of the cross arm. Visitors to Versailles could observe many types of boats, from small dinghies to elegant yachts, plying the waters of the Grand Canal. Colbert commissioned a fleet of scaled-down warships to sail in the canal, a demonstration to all who saw them of France's status as an emerging naval power.

The Trianons

Versailles was built to be a refuge for Louis XIV, a place where he could leave behind the burdens of royal life in Paris. But political pressures inevitably followed the king to his country palace, and he soon longed for an even more secluded and less formal retreat on the grounds of Versailles. Escaping politics, however, was not his only motivation for desiring a private sanctuary. It also allowed Louis and his favorite mistress, Françoise Athénaïs de Rochechouart de Mortemart, marquise de Montespan, a place for private romantic interludes.

Originally designed by Le Vau, the initial building, called the Porcelain Trianon, was completed in 1670. The name *Trianon* came from the small town razed to make room for the building. *Porcelain* described the blue and white tiles that adorned its exterior, an example of the growing interest of the era in Chinese designs. The Porcelain Trianon stood for only seventeen years. In 1687 Louis ordered a new, larger château built in its place. Mansart designed the new Grand Trianon in the style of Italian architecture. It was twice the size of the Porcelain Trianon and was built mainly of marble from the Languedoc region in southern France (thus its original name, the Marble Trianon). The architect himself described it as "a little pink marble and porphyry [a purple-hued crystalline rock] palace with delightful gardens."[30] The single-story Grand Trianon held private apartments for the king and his family and included a gallery 98 feet (30 m) long and a peristyle, an open colonnade or porch, facing a formal garden on the west side of the building. Flowers surrounded the building, creating a colorful and aromatic atmosphere for those visiting and living in the informal palace.

A similar but more modest retreat was built by Louis's successor,

The water-spouting frogs of Versailles's Latona Basin illustrate a myth dedicated to Latona, the mother of the god Apollo. In the fountain's center is a marble sculpture of Latona, Apollo, and his twin sister Diana.

his grandson Louis XV. The Petit Trianon, begun around 1762, was a gift from Louis XV to his mistress, Madame de Pompadour. Architect Ange-Jacques Gabriel designed the classic Greek-style structure with a square floor plan and a simple, classically proportioned limestone exterior, placing Corinthian columns and pilasters along the outer facade. Inside, the ground floor held service spaces such as the kitchen, while on the main floor, with its large rectangular windows, were the public spaces, the dining room, and the bedroom suite. An interesting detail of the dining room was the idea of installing a pulley system to raise the table from the kitchen directly below, thus eliminating the need for dining servants. While it was a unique idea, it was never completed.

Madame de Pompadour was never able to enjoy the Petit Trianon, as she died four years before its completion in 1768. Louis himself died six years later. Louis XVI gave the château to his queen, Marie-Antoinette, in 1774, and it is with her that the building is most identified. Although she had the Petit Trianon completely renovated, the queen was not satisfied with just her small retreat; she wanted a whole village. The Hameau de la Reine (the Queen's Hamlet) was an idealized reproduction of a French peasant village built around a small lake next to the Petit Trianon. Complete with a working dairy, a mill, rustic thatch-roofed cottages, and a house for the queen, it was a place where Marie-Antoinette could relax in a rustic setting and play the part of a peasant. Such frivolous play-acting on the part of the queen did nothing to endear her to the peasants, who rightly blamed the royals for the real hardships they were forced to endure.

André Le Nôtre's gardens at Versailles earned him an international reputation as the seventeenth century's premiere landscape designer. When he died in 1700, even the irascible Saint-Simon praised him:

He was illustrious as having been the first designer of those beautiful gardens which adorn France, and which, indeed, have so surpassed the gardens of Italy, that the most famous masters of that country come here to admire and learn. Le Notre had a probity [integrity], an exactitude, and an uprightness which made him esteemed and loved by everybody.[31]

CHAPTER FOUR

Life at Versailles

Nicolas Fouquet's unwise but lavish fete of August 17, 1661, ultimately led to his downfall, but it also provided Louis XIV with an inspiration for hosting a grand party of his own. In 1664 Louis was twenty-six years old; Mazarin had been gone for three years, and Louis had asserted his determination to rule France as absolute monarch. Many histories quote Louis as declaring, *"L'État c'est moi"*—"I am the state." Whether he actually said this or not is uncertain, but there is no doubt that he believed it. And now was the time to show France, and the world, that he meant it.

His first fete was called Les Plaisirs de l'Ile Enchantée, or the Pleasures of the Enchanted Isle. Although officially organized in honor of Louis's mother, Anne of Austria, and his wife, Marie-Thérèse, it was a poorly kept secret that the real honoree was Louis's current favorite mistress, Louise de La Val-

> **WORDS IN CONTEXT**
> jousting
> *Combat or exhibition where knights attack their opponents on horseback with lances.*

lière. In addition, the fete would display the Sun King's radiance for all to see and introduce his building campaigns at Versailles. Louis planned and executed the festivities with his typical attention to detail. The gardens became the theater in which the entertainments of the weeklong fete were held. The theme of the Pleasures of the Enchanted Isle was based on an epic sixteenth-century Italian poem in which a sorceress holds a knight named Ruggiero and his men captive on an enchanted island. Louis, always a lover of the theatrical arts, played the part of Ruggiero. Historian Pincas describes the pageantry of the fete's opening night:

> At about six in the evening the spectacle commenced with a procession led by the herald of arms followed by three pages, four trumpeters and two drummers. Next came the king as Ruggiero . . . followed by the nobles of the kingdom, who advancing two by two, acted the part of Ruggiero's suite. . . . All the knights and their horses were magnificently arrayed. Louis XIV wore a breastplate of cloth-of-silver covered with gold embroidery and diamonds; the plumes on his helmet were flame red and his horse's harness gleamed with gold, silver and precious stones.[32]

For the first three nights of the festivities, Versailles's gardens were transformed into a fairytale landscape illuminated with thousands of lights. The six hundred guests were entertained with the story of Ruggiero and his knights told in dance, music, and fantastic stage settings. On the third night the drama ended with a spectacular fireworks display. The fete continued for the rest of the week with jousting exhibitions, tours of the gardens, lotteries, and more theatrical performances. With the end of the festivities, the guests went home and Louis, satisfied that he had provided his guests with a grand experience, returned to the royal palace at Fontainebleau (the court would not move permanently to Versailles for another eighteen years).

WORDS IN CONTEXT
hierarchy
A system of ranking groups of people.

Four years later Louis organized another spectacular fete called the Grand Divertissement Royal, or the Grand Royal Entertainment, to celebrate France's victory in its recent war with Spain. Once again the gardens provided the background for the entertainment, which was held on July 18, 1668. The guests, this time numbering some fifteen hundred, were enthralled with music, dance, plays, and tours of the gardens. A sumptuous buffet was laid out in the gardens, after

Members of the French aristocracy enjoy themselves at a grand party at the Palace of Versailles. Louis XIV hosted a truly extravagant celebration at his palace in 1664—a week-long party that boasted six hundred guests.

which a grand ball was held in an octagonal outdoor room designed by Le Vau. The evening concluded with a dazzling fireworks display that lit up the night sky with Louis's royal monogram.

The Grand Divertissement Royal was an impressive exhibition of Louis's burgeoning wealth and power. But although the lavish festivities eventually came to an end, the routine of daily life as the king of France at Versailles remained.

The King's Routine

In 1682 Louis and his court took up permanent residence at Versailles. Life in the palace of the Sun King was one where elaborate codes of etiquette, a strict social hierarchy, and ceremonial tradition ruled everything that happened at Versailles. The daily routine of the king was so predictable that Saint-Simon remarked, "Give me an almanac and a watch, and even if I am three hundred leagues away from him I will tell you what the King is doing."[33]

The daily routine began with the *lever*, the ceremonial rising of the king. At 8:00 a.m. attendants entered the king's bedchamber to begin the daily ritual with the *petit levée*. It was a great honor to be selected as part of the king's rising ceremony. Several attendants went to the fireplace to light the fire, while another opened the shutters; then the *valet de chambre* gently roused the king with a whispered, "Sire, it is time."[34] When the bed curtains were opened, Louis's official day began. He was briefly examined by a physician, shaved by a barber (every other day), and given assistance with choosing his attire for the day (including his wig, selected from a collection of hundreds).

After a simple breakfast, Louis attended mass in the Royal Chapel and then spent the rest of the morning in his apartment for consultations with his ministers on various aspects of the nation's business: finance, foreign policy, and the progress of the ongoing construction work at Versailles. At 1:00 p.m. Louis returned to his cabinet for the midday meal, or *couvert*, named after the French word for "covered," as the king's food was served in covered dishes to keep it warm. Saint-Simon describes the *couvert*:

> The King ate by himself in his chamber upon a square table in front of the middle window. It was more or less abundant, for he ordered in the morning whether it was to be "a little," or "very little" service. But even at this last, there were always many dishes, and three courses without counting the fruit. The dinner being ready, the principal courtiers entered; then all who were known; and the gentleman of the chamber on duty informed the King.[35]

Louis XIV had a healthy appetite, which Princess Palatine, his sister-in-law, described in detail: "I have often seen the King eat four plates of soup . . . a whole pheasant, a partridge, a large plate of salad, two thick slices of ham, a dish of mutton . . . a plateful of pastries and then fruit and hard-boiled eggs."[36] Although the fork recently had been introduced to France, Louis disdained the implement, eating his meals with a knife and his hands.

The king's afternoons were often spent enjoying his favorite pastime, hunting, or sometimes taking a leisurely stroll through the

 THE KING AT COURT

No one wrote in more detail about life in the court of Louis XIV than Louis de Rouvroy, duc de Saint-Simon. In his *Mémoires*, Saint-Simon describes the king's painstaking attention to the members of his court:

> He was exceedingly jealous of the attention paid him. Not only did he notice the presence of the most distinguished courtiers, but those of inferior degree also. He looked to the right and to the left, not only upon rising but upon going to bed, at his meals, in passing through his apartments, or his gardens of Versailles, where alone the courtiers were allowed to follow him; he saw and noticed everybody; not one escaped him, not even those who hoped to remain unnoticed. He marked well all absentees from the Court, found out the reason of their absence, and never lost an opportunity of acting towards them as the occasion might seem to justify. With some of the courtiers (the most distinguished), it was a demerit not to make the Court their ordinary abode; with others 'twas a fault to come but rarely; for those who never or scarcely ever came it was certain disgrace. When their names were in any way mentioned, "I do not know them," the King would reply haughtily. Those who presented themselves but seldom were thus Characterise[d]: "They are people I never see;" these decrees were irrevocable.

Louis de Rouvroy, duc de Saint-Simon, *The Memoirs of Louis XIV and His Court and of the Regency—Complete*, Project Gutenberg, e-book no. 3875. www.gutenberg.org.

gardens. Early evening entertainment might include dancing, plays, concerts, and games of cards or billiards. At around 10:00 p.m. supper, the *grand couvert*, was held in the queen's antechamber, with his family sitting with him at the table, surrounded once more by members of the court. Finally, to end the king's day, a ceremony called the *coucher* ("lying down"), reversed the process of the morning's *lever*. Attendants helped Louis undress and prepare for bed, extinguished the candles, and retired from the king's bedchamber, leaving only the *valet de chambre* to sleep on a roll-out cot in the king's bedroom. It was around 11:30 p.m., and the halls of Versailles fell silent. At sunrise the next day, the ritual would begin all over again.

The Grandeur of Versailles

Although the king's daily life was one of unchanging formality and etiquette, the backdrop for his routine was spectacular. Of all the royal palaces throughout Europe, Versailles was without equal in its interior design and decoration. Most of the credit for this goes to painter Charles Le Brun. At fifteen years of age, Le Brun was painting on commission from Cardinal Richelieu, Louis XIII's chief minister. In 1646, after working for four years in Rome, Le Brun returned to France. He continued to receive commissions from many influential people, including Nicolas Fouquet, whose château of Vaux-le-Vicomte marked the beginning of Le Brun's association with Le Vau and Le Nôtre.

What Le Vau was to the architecture of Versailles and Le Nôtre was to the gardens, Le Brun was to the interior design of the palace. Every aspect of art at Versailles was under Le Brun's control. Author Nancy Mitford describes him as "a decorator of genius. He himself designed everything for the château, chairs, tables, carpets, panelling, silver and tapestries, even keyholes."[37] By 1662 Le Brun had been named the king's first painter and, along with Colbert, decided to decorate the rooms in the king's Grand Apartment in a planetary motif. Dominant in this scheme was the Salon d'Apollon and its association with the sun, Louis's royal symbol. In the other rooms of the apartment, the ceilings were painted with representations of gods associated with various planets. Mars, the Roman god of war, was depicted on the ceiling of the Salon de Mars. Other rooms included the salons of Mercury, Diana, and Venus. In the Queen's apartment, the ceilings were painted with scenes of ancient heroines in action.

In time, the planetary themes gave way to more earthly depictions. Louis eventually wanted the palace's art to reflect his transformation of France into the most important nation in the world. Since most visitors to Versailles, nobles and commoners alike, passed through the Hall of Mirrors, it was the most important location for Le Brun's artwork portraying Louis XIV in all his glory. The central ceiling panel depicts Louis XIV, garbed in Roman armor, assuming absolute power in France. In the Hall of Mirrors,

> [its] seventy-three metres [240 ft] glorified the political, economic and artistic success of France. Political success is demonstrated by thirty compositions in the [ceiling] arch painted by Le Brun, which illustrate the glorious history of Louis XIV in the first eighteen years of his government, from 1661 until the Peace of Nijmegen [1678–79]. Military and diplomatic victories, as well as reforms in view of the reorganisation of the kingdom, are portrayed in the form of antique allegories.[38]

These themes were repeated throughout the palace in sculpture, paintings, and tapestries. As Louis had desired, Versailles had become, according to historian Tony Spawforth, "a new benchmark of artistic excellence"[39] and an example to the world. And people from all over the world came to see what life was like in the king's palace.

Palace Life

"If there is anything singular about the French monarchy, it is the free and easy access which the subjects have to their prince,"[40] wrote Louis XIV in his memoirs. Of course, the influential people who possessed invitations to the various fetes hosted by the king were well received. The public was not barred from entering the palace at other times, as

ACQVISITION DE DVNKERQVE

A close-up view of the ceiling painting within the Hall of Mirrors shows the detail that went into the artwork of Charles Le Brun. Most visitors to Versailles passed through the hall and therefore could not miss the artist's depictions of the French king in all his glory.

the gates were usually open from 6:00 a.m. to midnight. Even a visitors' guide, now lost to history, was published. But there were some restrictions: for example, a dress code required male visitors to wear a sword, a sign of nobility. This proved not much of a hindrance, however, as those who lacked the appropriate weapon could simply rent one at the front gate before entering the palace. Visitors wandered the palace, hoping to get a glimpse of the king. As they strolled through the gardens they often trampled delicate flowerbeds or plucked flowers or tree branches to keep as souvenirs.

Aside from the king and his family, the king's court made up the majority of the residents of Versailles. By living at the palace, they surrendered their political power to the king, and they soon learned that to retain the favor of the king they must strive to be seen. As Louis walked through the halls of Versailles, courtiers waited patiently for the chance to have a word with the king or pass a paper petition to him. Once the king appeared, approaching him could be daunting. According to Saint-Simon, "one had to get used to the King's appearance if one did not want to feel awed into silence when talking to him."[41] Such attempts at engaging the king were not always successful. One judge presented a petition to the king, who placed the paper in his pocket. Later, the judge spoke of his good fortune to another courtier: "When I told him I had handed over my petition to the King at his command, he said: 'Your audience was completely wasted: when the King changes his clothes this afternoon, before going hunting, the petition will remain in the pocket of the first coat, and it will be as good as lost.'"[42]

WORDS IN CONTEXT

guillotine

A device used for capital punishment during the French Revolution, consisting of a vertical frame and a weighted blade for beheading rivals.

Living in such a beautiful palace, surrounded by great works of art, might seem to be an ideal existence. But courtiers soon learned that the reality was something less than perfect. As large as the palace was, accommodations for most of the nobles consisted of small, cramped rooms, often having neither a window nor a fireplace. According to Mitford, "Hundreds of courtiers were crammed into the Nobles' or north wing of the château. It was a maze of corridors, where strangers lost their way hopelessly. People could live here for years, forgotten by everybody."[43] Even the hallways of the palace were crowded with courtiers in sedan chairs (chairs carried by servants) jamming the corridors. Nobles could rent these chairs but were not allowed to own them. It was expensive to live at Versailles as well, in no small part due to the gambling that took place at the palace. Gaming was a fashionable way for the nobles to while away idle hours, and it kept them too occupied to plot against the king. Whether playing cards, games with dice, or billiards, nobles were expected to win (or lose) with the grace befitting their station.

With the constant building at Versailles, noise and construction dirt made life at the palace less than pleasant. Fireplaces also created soot that accumulated on the walls and furniture. With all the nobles, servants, and visitors crowding into the palace, sanitation was, not surprisingly, an ongoing problem. Today's concept of the bathroom did not exist in seventeenth-century France. Chamber pots were placed strategically around the palace in hallways and stairwells, and privies (a type of outhouse) were located around the gardens. Unpleasant odors were common in the palace, not only from the chamber pots but also from the people themselves. Bathing was not a common activity at the time, and copious amounts of perfume were used to cover body odor. Heat and cold also took a toll on the residents of Versailles. Summers in the cramped quarters were stifling, and taking refuge in the cool bosquets of the gardens was the only way to find relief from the heat. In the winter Versailles's fireplaces were inadequate at best, and constant drafts made much of the palace frigid and uncomfortable. Saint-Simon recalls an icicle falling into his teacup, even though he was sitting directly in front of a fireplace.

Versailles After Louis XIV

At the death of Louis XIV in 1715, his successor and great-grandson, Louis XV, was only five years old. A week after his great-grandfather's death, while Louis XIV's body still lay in Versailles, the young heir to the throne was taken to live in Paris. He would not see Versailles again for seven years. When he returned on June 15, 1722, the twelve-year-old king was greeted by a cheering crowd; after praying in the Royal Chapel, he took a walking tour of the gardens and visited the

TAKING FLIGHT AT VERSAILLES

During the late seventeenth century a movement that came to be known as the Enlightenment was beginning, stimulating countless advances in philosophy, politics, and the sciences. In 1666 Louis XIV ordered the creation of the Académie des Sciences (Academy of Sciences) in Paris to advise the king on all manner of scientific inquiry. Under the supervision of Jean-Baptiste Colbert, the academy held discussions of topics of current interest and sponsored scientific expeditions.

In 1783 Versailles was the site of a scientific milestone: the first aerostatic (propelled by air rather than motion) flight. Two brothers, Jacques-Etienne and Joseph-Michel Montgolfier, had been experimenting with hot air balloons for a year, achieving success with small paper and cloth apparatuses they called *ballons*. After more successful tests, the academy asked the brothers to demonstrate a larger balloon at Versailles. On September 19, 1783, they prepared to launch a brightly decorated balloon measuring 60.4 feet (18.4 m) tall and 43.5 feet (13.3 m) wide from the forecourt of Versailles. In a basket beneath the balloon were history's first air passengers—a rooster, a duck, and a sheep. Under the watchful eyes of Louis XVI, Marie-Antoinette, and a crowd of courtiers, the balloon rose 1,500 feet (457.2 m) and remained airborne for eight minutes, landing safely about 2.17 miles (3.5 km) from the palace.

The Montgolfier brothers continued to experiment and refine their design, culminating in the first hot air balloon flight carrying human passengers on November 21, 1783.

Hall of Mirrors. There he lay down on the floor, perhaps tired from his long jaunt, but also obtaining a good vantage point from which to view Le Brun's masterwork on the ceiling. Once he had settled in at the palace, his daily routine was much like that of Louis XIV, although at times he would change the hour of his *lever*, allowing him to sleep later if the previous night had kept him up.

Life in the palace under the new king was in many ways comparable to that under his great-grandfather's reign. Etiquette still ruled the conduct of the court. The hallways of Versailles still bustled with the comings and goings of courtiers and their entourages. The king still hosted grand fetes for his elegantly attired guests and presented plays and spectacular fireworks displays. But beneath the facade of glittering parties and court formalities, attitudes toward the French monarchy were undergoing a change.

The costs of running a nation and the upkeep of the palace fell squarely on the shoulders of the French citizens. Adding the costs of pursuing the king's wars squeezed his subjects even tighter. Taxes on everything from income to such necessary items as soap, tobacco, and salt took about half of a typical French citizen's earnings. While sumptuous feasts were served in Versailles, the common man had little money to feed his family. While visiting the country, an Italian ambassador fittingly described the disparity between noble and commoner when he wrote, "In France, nine-tenths of the people die of hunger, one-tenth of indigestion."[44] Even within the court, discontent grew as respect for the king was beginning to decline. Scandalous pamphlets, poems, songs, and drawings circulated that criticized the king for taking as his mistress a commoner, Madame de Pompadour.

On January 5, 1757, Louis XV was eager to spend some private time at the Grand Trianon. As he was leaving the palace, a man leapt from the shadows and, avoiding the guards surrounding Louis, attacked the king. "Someone has struck me hard with his elbow,"[45] the king exclaimed. But when he felt his side, his hand came away bloody. The stab wound bled profusely, but it was superficial and not life threatening. Louis recovered, and his would-be assassin, a man named Robert-François Damiens, who seems to have blamed the king for religious problems in France, was executed. It was the first time in more than 150 years that anyone had dared try to kill a French king.

Louis lived seventeen years after the assassination attempt, eventually succumbing to smallpox at Versailles on May 10, 1774. His grandson, Louis XVI, inherited the throne and a nation deeply in debt. His reign would be the last absolute monarchy in France, and he would die not of disease but at the hands of a revolutionary mob.

Louis XVI appears on the balcony at Versailles in October 1789 to tell the angry Parisian mob that he will return to Paris. Three years later the king and his family were arrested and imprisoned; Louis and his wife Marie-Antoinette were executed in 1793.

Revolution

In France's ancien régime, the population was divided into three estates, or classes: the First Estate (clergy), the Second Estate (nobles), and the Third Estate (the common people). Around 27 million people, or 97 percent of the French population, belonged to the Third Estate, which included peasants, craftsmen, farmers, merchants, and other ordinary citizens. Each estate was represented in the États-General, or General Assembly, and each had one vote. Thus, if the minority classes of clergy and nobles voted alike on legislation, they effectively nullified the wishes of the vast majority of the citizenry. In a pamphlet published in January 1789, entitled "What Is the Third Estate?," the author answered his own question: "Everything; but an everything shackled and oppressed."[46]

When the États-General met at Versailles the next June, Louis ordered the representatives of the Third Estate locked out of the meeting chamber. Withdrawing to a nearby indoor tennis court, the banished delegates declared themselves to be the National Assembly, vowing to remain in session until a new constitution was established. This "Tennis Court Oath" fanned revolutionary fever in France, prompting the Grand Peur, or Great Fear, in late July and early August. Peasants formed armed militias to counter a possible crackdown of the rebellion by the king. On July 14 approximately one thousand rebels stormed the Bastille, a fortress prison in Paris, to secure ammunition for their weapons. The French Revolution had begun, and Paris was in turmoil. Versailles was still a calm refuge for Louis XVI and his court, but that tranquility would not last long. On October 5 a mob of women marched from Paris to Versailles to protest the lack of bread for their families. Gathering supporters along the way, the crowd eventually invaded the palace and forced Louis and his queen, Marie-Antoinette, to return to Paris. For a time, the king appeared to accept the reforms demanded by the Third Estate, but eventually he lost the trust of the revolutionaries. Louis and his family were arrested on August 13, 1792, and imprisoned in the Temple, a medieval castle in Paris far removed from the elegant environs of Versailles.

The Third Estate eventually got what they had fought so long for: the monarchy was overthrown and France's First Republic was established in September 1792. On January 21, 1793, Louis XVI was convicted of treason and went under the guillotine in a public execution in the Place de la Révolution in Paris. Marie-Antoinette suffered the same fate on October 16. Although the king was gone, Versailles, the symbol of all the excesses of the monarchy, remained.

CHAPTER FIVE

Versailles in the Modern Era

For the first time in more than a century, Versailles was no longer the king's residence. Paris once again became the seat of French government. Without a royal family and its court to occupy it, Versailles had become nothing more than a magnificent but empty shell. Furnishings from the palace were sold at public auction; people bought cabinets, gold clocks, dressing tables, tapestries, even curtains and chandeliers, at bargain prices. Visitors still came to Versailles to wander the empty halls left abandoned by the last of the Bourbon kings. But the cost of keeping up a vast edifice that served no useful purpose was impractical. Although the most radical of the French revolutionaries advocated tearing down the palace, most French citizens could not bring themselves to consider such a drastic measure. Those who lived near the palace felt a special loyalty to it, believing that Versailles, even in its present state, was essential to the local economy. At one point consideration was given to either renting or selling the palace to bring in revenue.

Although Versailles may have been empty of occupants, it was still filled with marvelous works of art. By the end of Louis XVI's reign, some twenty-five hundred paintings adorned the walls of the palace. A museum would be the ideal setting to display such a splendid collection, and by the middle of the eighteenth century there had been several proposals to establish a royal museum in Paris. In 1791

⬡ UNESCO WORLD HERITAGE SITE

The ruins of archaeological treasures, such as the Parthenon in Greece, remind us that man and time take a toll on historic monuments. In 1972 the United Nations Educational, Scientific and Cultural Organization (UNESCO) adopted a treaty designed to "encourage the identification, protection and preservation of cultural and natural heritage around the world considered to be of outstanding value to humanity." As of 2013, the World Heritage List included 981 sites of cultural and natural importance throughout the world.

The palace and gardens of Versailles were added to the list in 1979, joining such famous monuments as Stonehenge in England, India's Taj Mahal, and Yellowstone National Park in the United States. Along with its corporate and government partners, UNESCO works to preserve its listed monuments from the ravages of pollution, urban spread, political unrest, natural disasters, and war. Along with helping to fund preservation efforts, UNESCO also supports educational experiences as well. For example, those who cannot visit Versailles in person can take a virtual online tour of the palace and gardens thanks to an alliance between UNESCO and the popular Internet search site Google.

Throughout its history, Versailles has endured the whims of its monarchs, a bloody revolution, and a devastating storm. It has survived them all. As a member of the UNESCO World Heritage List, the palace faces a future protected from whatever man and nature can bring against it.

UNESCO, "World Heritage." http://whc.unesco.org.

the National Assembly declared that the Louvre in Paris would be "a place for bringing together all the sciences and the arts."[47] In 1793 the Musée Central des Arts (Central Museum of the Arts) was founded at the Louvre. It opened to the public on August 10, 1793 (almost one year to the day since Louis XVI was arrested), and included numerous works of art taken from Versailles, including Leonardo da Vinci's

Mona Lisa. Around the same time, all of the furniture in the palace was sold at auction to raise money for the government. After years of debate over what to do with Versailles, the palace was officially preserved for future generations. On May 5, 1794, the National Assembly declared that Versailles "should be preserved and kept up at the public expense for the enjoyment of the people, and for establishments useful to agriculture and the arts."[48]

With this decree, Versailles gained a second life. Instead of a palace to indulge the whims of kings and queens, it became a place of learning and culture. Historian Francis Loring Payne describes the new Versailles:

> The institutions whose establishment at Versailles definitely saved the chateau and its dependencies for posterity, were, at the Palace, a conservatory of arts and sciences and a library of 30,000 volumes; in the Kitchen Garden a school of gardening and husbandry; at the Grand Commune, a manufactory of arms; at the Menagerie, a school of agriculture. Halls that had echoed to the dance and the clink of gold at gaming-tables now heard profound lectures on history, ancient languages, mathematics, chemistry, and political economy! Classic exercises beneath the painted ceilings of these memoried rooms! Scholastic discourse where music and laughter had vibrated for a hundred extravagant years![49]

The Museum of Versailles

When numerous paintings were removed from Versailles and taken to the Louvre's Central Museum of the Arts, many people became concerned that the palace was losing too much of the exquisite art that had made it great. In 1797 the National Assembly decided that Versailles would be the location of the Musée Spécial de l'Ecole Française (Special Museum of the French School) to showcase the works of French artists. The Louvre retained works of art from foreign nations, but Versailles received all of the paintings by French artists. About six hundred French paintings soon adorned the walls of the palace.

The museum officially opened in 1801 but closed in 1806, and its best works were again removed and distributed to other royal residences across France. Two years earlier, Napoléon Bonaparte had been crowned Emperor Napoléon I, inaugurating the First Empire in France. As emperor, Napoléon desired a residence suitable for his position, so naturally Versailles came to mind. He had plans made for the renovation of the palace, but the restoration and maintenance expenses were too great. Instead, Napoléon decided to use the Grand Trianon as a summer retreat. Neglected since the end of the revolution, Napoléon had the building restored beginning in 1805. When Napoléon was not abroad fighting wars, he stayed at the Trianon with his family.

When Napoléon's rule ended in 1814, the Bourbon line of kings was restored as a constitutional monarchy, beginning with the short reigns of Louis XVIII and Charles X. In 1830 Louis-Philippe ascended to the throne, becoming "the King of the French," a title that declared he would rule with the best interests of his subjects in mind. To solidify his commitment to unite the people of France, Louis-Philippe introduced the idea of establishing a history museum at Versailles. "The aim," writes historian Spawforth, "was to create a symbol of unity that would bring together a politically fractured France in the memory of national glories."[50] Opened in 1837, the Museum of French History was dedicated "*A toutes les gloires de la France*" ("To all the glories of France"), a phrase that can still be seen inscribed on the palace's facade. The museum displayed huge paintings illustrating the history of France; artwork depicting the momentous battles waged throughout French history was especially prominent in a new room called the Gallery of Battles.

Although the art displayed was impressive, the palace itself had to be altered to accommodate it. For example, Louis-Philippe had his architect demolish the apartments located in the south wing to

Emperor Napoléon Bonaparte of France used the Grand Trianon (pictured, along with the grounds in front of it) as a summer retreat. He restored the structure, which had fallen into disrepair after the French Revolution.

create the 394-foot-long (120 m) Gallery of Battles. People came to Versailles from all over France to marvel at the Museum of French History's treasures. But in 1848 a revolution inaugurated the Second Empire, removing Louis-Philippe from power and installing Charles-Louis-Napoléon Bonaparte as Emperor Napoléon III.

The Museum of French History was filled with art glorifying past military victories of the French army, particularly those won under Napoléon I. During the 1870s another war raged, but this time France faced a humiliating defeat, and Versailles played a part in its conclusion.

Versailles in War and Peace

As absolute monarch, Louis XIV had made France the most powerful nation in Europe. By 1870 a new threat had grown to imperil the nation. Napoléon III was troubled by the rising power of Prussia and its plan to create a formidable German empire. In July 1870 the emperor declared war on the German kingdom, beginning the Franco-Prussian War. Napoléon, confident of an easy victory, took command of the French army. But he lacked the military skills that his uncle, Napoléon I, had employed with great success. Napoléon was captured on September 2, 1870, and two weeks later Prussian troops besieged Paris, causing widespread starvation. The seat of government was once again moved to Versailles. With its emperor in exile and its capital city surrounded, France ultimately surrendered.

In December 1870 German delegates met in the Hall of Mirrors at Versailles to proclaim the creation of the empire of Germany. In an ironic twist of fate, the hall rang with the delegates' cheers as they celebrated beneath paintings depicting France's past victories over Germany. On February 26, 1871, the Treaty of Versailles was signed by delegates of France and the German Empire, ending the Franco-Prussian War. It marked the end of the Second Empire and the creation of the Third Republic.

Forty-three years later, Germany and France were embroiled in another war, this one of global proportions. World War I, known at the time as the Great War, was the most devastating armed conflict the world had ever seen. In four years of bloody fighting more than 37 million soldiers were killed, wounded, or missing. At the end of this bloodbath, the Hall of Mirrors again played its part in the process of restoring the peace. The Paris Peace Conference began at Versailles on January 19, 1919, to work out the details of a treaty that the delegates hoped would produce a lasting peace. On June 28 the new Treaty of Versailles was ready to be signed. British delegate Sir Harold Nicolson described the scene at the time:

> We enter the Galerie des Glaces (Hall of Mirrors). It is divided into three sections. At the far end are the Press already thickly installed. In the middle there is a horse-shoe table for the plenipotentiaries. In front of that; like a guillotine, is the table for the signatures. It is supposed to be raised on a dais but, if so, the dais can be but a few inches high. . . . There must be seats for over a thousand persons. This robs the ceremony of all privilege and therefore of all dignity.[51]

The Hall of Mirrors was hushed as the German representatives signed the treaty. Within the elegant chambers of Versailles, a brutal war had been ended. As they left the palace, the delegates dared to hope that the Treaty of Versailles would usher in a future without war. They could not know that their hopes would be dashed twenty years later with the beginning of World War II.

Restoring the Palace

Versailles had served as a museum for decades, but Pierre de Nolhac was about to change that. Born in 1859, Nolhac was a scholar and writer who first visited Versailles in 1878. Wandering through the palace, he was struck by the beauty and magnificence of Versailles, writing in his diary, *"Ce que j'ai vu de plus beau à Paris, c'est Versailles."*[52] ("What I've seen [of] the most beautiful in Paris, it is Versailles.") In 1892 Nolhac became the chief curator of the museum, setting as his goal the restoration of the palace to the way it was during the reign of

Louis XIV. He began by reversing the changes that Louis-Philippe had made to the palace, restoring woodwork to its original state and bringing back furniture that had been removed. Nolhac sorted through the art collection and rearranged the displays, and he also established a new policy for acquiring more works of art. He reorganized Versailles's administration, which had allowed the palace to fall into disrepair. Tourists once more began visiting Versailles.

Nolhac retired from his position as curator in 1920. As the first to make a priority of restoring Versailles in the nineteenth and twentieth centuries, Nolhac set the standard for those who would follow, including American oil tycoon John D. Rockefeller Jr. The billionaire son of the founder of Standard Oil, Rockefeller was appalled at the destruction of famous buildings in France after the Great War. In 1923 *Time* magazine reported that "the historic and beautiful palace of Versailles is in a state of decay and the marvelous fountains are breaking down."[53] The leaking palace roofs were especially in immediate need of repair. Through his charitable organization, the Rockefeller

Foundation, he donated some $2 million for the restoration of the palace and gardens (as well as the Rheims Cathedral and Fontainebleau Palace) between 1925 and 1928. As welcome as Rockefeller's donation was, it could not remedy all of the problems associated with a centuries-old structure.

By the mid-twentieth century Versailles was still in perilous condition. André Japy, chief architect at Versailles from 1940 to 1954, commented in 1951, "It is like a house of cards. If one part begins collapsing, everything else will follow. It is no longer a question of repairing one part of the building; everything must be restored."[54] One of the areas most in need of repair was the Royal Opera. Between 1952 and 1957 the opera house underwent a massive restoration begun by Japy and completed by his successor, Marc Saltet. Working from original plans, the architects restored the opera house to its original glory. In April 1957 the restored opera house opened with a celebration that included, among other guests, Queen Elizabeth II of England. The opera house was closed again between 2007 and 2009 for further work to bring its technical areas up to modern safety standards.

In 1963, after visits to Versailles from foreign dignitaries including President John F. Kennedy and First Lady Jackie Kennedy, French president Charles de Gaulle ordered the renovation of the Grand Trianon to accommodate future guests. De Gaulle also instructed that the north wing of the Grand Trianon be remodeled as a presidential suite. The building was in great need of modernization. André Malraux, the minister for cultural affairs under whose direction the restoration took place, wrote, "The task is considerable because it involves installing all modern amenities in a building which has no telephone line, heating, kitchen or bathroom. In 1963, the programme was expanded by the order from the President of the Republic for an additional suite of apartments reserved for the Head of State."[55] The

Restorers work in 2007 on chandeliers from Versailles's Hall of Mirrors. The extensive renovations restored the original luster to artwork and gilt decorations, woodwork, parquet floors, chandeliers, and mirrors.

⬡ SUMMIT AT VERSAILLES

Exactly three hundred years after Louis XIV installed his government at Versailles, a group of international leaders met there to discuss the world's economy. On June 4, 1982, seven heads of non-Communist countries assembled at Versailles. Known as G7, the group represented the seven wealthiest nations in the Western world: the United States, France, Great Britain, Japan, West Germany, Italy, and Canada. Hosted by French president François Mitterrand, the delegates, including US president Ronald Reagan, stayed at the Grand Trianon during the two-day conference.

The meetings took place in the Coronation Room, a chamber that originally had been a chapel and was then converted to a room for the king's and queen's guards. Under the room's gilded ceiling, the delegates sat around a large conference table, enduring the stifling heat in the room as well as some tension between the attendees. The meetings dealt with such issues as interest rates, international financial and trade cooperation, rising inflation, and the recession that affected many of the countries. Between sessions, meals were served at the Garden Salon of the Trianon. At the summit's conclusion, the delegates enjoyed a sumptuous dinner in the Hall of Mirrors, a performance in the Royal Opera, and, reminiscent of Louis XIV's grand fetes, a spectacular fireworks display.

The closing ceremony marked the end of a conference that made little progress in solving the world's economic problems. But for a few days Versailles once more had been the background against which international relations were deliberated.

newly restored Grand Trianon opened in 1966 and was active as a guest residence throughout the 1960s and 1970s.

The Hall of Mirrors underwent a renovation in 2007. Working in one half of the hall at a time to keep it open to visitors, some one hundred restorers cleaned the artwork and gilt decorations, restored woodwork, and installed a new parquet floor. The diverse aspects of the hall, from paintings and sculptures to architectural elements and electrical systems, required skilled specialists to perform the work. Naturally, special attention was paid to the restoration of the hall's key component: the mirrors. Of the 357 mirrors that line the east wall, only 48 had to be replaced—and not one was broken in the process. "Some mirrors were replaced in the early 19th century," commented Vincent Guerre, who did the restoration work on the mirrors, "but 60 percent of these mirrors were there under Louis XIV. This is a magical place, a testimony to an era."[56]

The Petit Trianon also was restored in a one-year project begun in 2007. The renovation work was designed to bring the building back to the time when Marie-Antoinette made it her royal home. Original furniture, which had been scattered across Europe, was located and purchased to furnish the building, and the interiors were restored to their Louis XVI–era condition. The Petit Trianon was reopened to the public on October 2, 2008, the first time the entire building was available for tourists to explore and enjoy.

A Devastating Storm

On the night of December 25, 1999, as the people of Western Europe were enjoying their Christmas celebrations, a catastrophic storm struck the region. France was the hardest hit, with ninety people killed and millions of francs in property damage incurred. Winds in excess of 130 miles per hour (209.2 km/h) damaged many historic structures, including Notre Dame Cathedral in Paris. The storm did not spare Versailles: the hurricane-force winds pummeled the palace for two hours. The next morning, the damage to the palace was clear. Dozens of windows had been broken and numerous lead roof tiles were peeled away. But it was the gardens that suffered the most damage from the storm. Ten thousand trees in the Versailles gardens were uprooted or snapped in two. Eighty percent of these trees were of rare species, and a few had unique historic significance, including two tulip trees planted for Marie-Antoinette, and Napoléon's Corsican pine tree dating to 1810. "The storm is a catastrophe without precedent," said French prime minister Lionel Jospin. "It was an exceptional, cataclysmic event with massive consequences."[57]

There was, however, some good amid all the destruction. Many of the uprooted trees were already scheduled for replacement. Pierre-André Lablaude, the chief architect, noted that "the trees that were blown down had been planted between 1860 and 1880. They were approaching the end of their lives and they were fragile." A replanting program was established, funded by a subsidy from the state as well as donations solicited from the public. Between 1999 and 2004, fifty thousand trees were planted in the Versailles gardens. The storm provided an opportunity not only to replace the destroyed trees but also to return the gardens to their original state. "We realized that the form of the garden had altered a lot with time," explained Lablaude. "We therefore decided to plant slow-growing species that would permit us to have a lower tree cover, and less overshadowed paths corresponding to the configuration of the small park at Versailles as Louis XIV knew it."[58]

Celebrating Versailles

Although its role as a royal residence has long since ended, Versailles continues to be a vital part of French culture and international tourism. The palace today is as lively as it was in the days of Louis XIV. The newly restored Royal Opera continues to present the kinds of concerts, operas, and ballets that once delighted the kings of France. In 2003 the Academy of Equestrian Arts was established in the Grand Stables at Versailles to train horses in the art of dressage as well as in such other disciplines as artistic fencing and Kyudo, or traditional Japanese archery. The Research Center of the Palace of Versailles conducts archaeological research and hosts symposiums and seminars on European history. Founded in 1988, the Baroque Music Center of Versailles organizes concerts, performs research, and provides higher education in the music of the Baroque era.

The Palace of Versailles and its illustrious gardens continue to be a vital part of French culture and tourism. It remains a monument to the splendor of France's past.

Versailles's role as a museum continues, annually hosting some 6 million visitors who marvel at the outstanding collection of paintings and sculptures as well as the architectural splendors of the palace itself and its beautiful gardens. The creator of those gardens, André Le Nôtre, was commemorated in 2013 with a yearlong celebration entitled "The Year of Le Nôtre." Marking the four-hundredth anniversary of Le Nôtre's birth, the palace paid tribute to the king's gardener with exhibitions highlighting his wide-ranging talents as landscaper, architect, hydraulics engineer, and city planner.

Throughout its nearly four-hundred-year history, Versailles has been many things: a modest hunting lodge, a museum, a king's palace, and a place where heads of state assembled to discuss the world's problems. Its halls have bustled with crowds of elegantly dressed courtiers seeking favors from the king. Those same halls were left empty and abandoned as the tide of politics turned more than once during its lifetime. But most of all, Versailles was, and always has been, a symbol. For Louis XIV, the Sun King, it was the symbol of his own magnificence and the all-encompassing power of an absolute monarch. For the peasants of eighteenth-century France, Versailles was a symbol of outrageous royal excess, and it became the target of revolutionaries who breached its sacred walls and destroyed the absolute monarchy once and for all. For delegates of the peace conferences who met in the Hall of Mirrors, it was a symbol of hope for a lasting peace in the world. Today that world sees Versailles for what it has always been—a monument to the splendor of past ages that, despite wars, unstable alliances, and physical neglect, still shines as the crown jewel of France.

SOURCE NOTES

Introduction: The Palace of the Sun King

1. Quoted in Veronica Buckley, *The Secret Wife of Louis XIV*. New York: Farrar, Straus, and Giroux, 2008, p. 258.
2. Quoted in Jean-Marie Pérouse de Montclos, *Versailles*. New York: Abbeville, 1991, p. 376.

Chapter One: The Hunting Lodge

3. Quoted in Guy Walton, *Louis XIV's Versailles*. Chicago: University of Chicago Press, 1986, p. 53.
4. Jacques Levron, *Daily Life at Versailles in the Sixteenth and Seventeenth Centuries*. New York: Macmillan, 1968, p.18.
5. Louis de Rouvroy, duc de Saint-Simon, *Versailles, the Court, and Louis XIV*, ed. and trans. Lucy Norton. New York: Harper & Row, 1966, p. 253.
6. Quoted in Pérouse de Montclos, *Versailles*, p. 25.
7. Quoted in Jean-Yves Dufour and Jean-Claude Le Guillou, "The Enclosure Wall of Louis XIII's Versailles Residence," *Antiquity*, vol. 82, no. 315, March 2008. www.antiquity.ac.uk.
8. Levron, *Daily Life at Versailles in the Sixteenth and Seventeenth Centuries*, p. 21.
9. Quoted in Pérouse de Montclos, *Versailles*, p. 30.
10. Quoted in Pérouse de Montclos, *Versailles*, p. 87.
11. Louis de Rouvroy, duc de Saint-Simon, *Memoirs of Louis XIV and His Court and of the Regency—Complete*, Project Gutenberg, e-book no. 3875. www.gutenberg.org.
12. Quoted in Antonia Fraser, *Love and Louis XIV: The Women in the Life of the Sun King*. New York: Doubleday, 2006, p. 12.
13. Quoted in Fraser, *Love and Louis XIV*, p. 18.
14. Victor Lucien Tapié, *France in the Age of Louis XIII and Richelieu*. Cambridge, UK: Cambridge University Press, 1984, p. 89.

Chapter Two: Building the Palace of Versailles

15. Quoted in Christopher Martin, *Louis XIV*. East Sussex, UK: Wayland, 1975, p. 17.
16. Quoted in Martin, *Louis XIV*, p. 18.
17. Quoted in Levron, *Daily Life at Versailles in the Sixteenth and Seventeenth Centuries*, p. 25.
18. Quoted in Vincent Cronin, *Louis XIV*. St. James's Place, England: Collins, 1964, p. 116.
19. Quoted in James Eugene Farmer, *Versailles and the Court Under Louis XIV*. New York: Century, 1905, p. 4.
20. Quoted in Pérouse de Montclos, *Versailles*, p. 92.
21. Farmer, *Versailles and the Court Under Louis XIV*, p. 23.
22. Quoted in Pierre-André Lablaude, *The Gardens of Versailles*. London: Zwemmer, 1995, p. 22.

Chapter Three: The Gardens of Versailles

23. Quoted in Pérouse de Montclos, *Versailles*, p. 27.
24. Quoted in Dana Thomas, "Château Vaux-le-Vicomte's Magisterial Gardens," *Daily AD* (blog), *Architectural Digest*, March 13, 2013. www.architecturaldigest.com.
25. Quoted in Ian Thompson, *The Sun King's Garden: Louis XIV, André Le Nôtre, and the Creation of the Gardens of Versailles*. New York: Bloomsbury, 2006, p. 88.
26. Quoted in Lablaude, *The Gardens of Versailles*, p. 22.
27. Francis Loring Payne, *The Story of Versailles*, Project Gutenberg, e-book no. 14857. www.gutenberg.org.
28. Stéphane Pincas, *Versailles: The History of the Gardens and Their Sculpture*. New York, NY: Thames and Hudson, 1996, p. 164.
29. Quoted in Thompson, *The Sun King's Garden*, p.139.
30. Quoted in Château de Versailles, "The Grand Trianon." http://en.chateauversailles.fr.
31. Saint-Simon, *The Memoirs of Louis XIV and His Court and of the Regency—Complete*.

Chapter Four: Life at Versailles

32. Quoted in Pincas, *Versailles*, p. 260.

33. Quoted in Maurice P. Ashley, *Louis XIV and the Greatness of France*. New York: Free, 1965, p. 23.

34. Quoted in Château de Versailles, "A Day in the Life of Louis XIV." http://en.chateauversailles.fr.

35. Saint-Simon, *The Memoirs of Louis XIV and His Court and of the Regency—Complete*.

36. Quoted in Gilette Ziegler, *At the Court of Versailles: Eye-Witness Reports from the Reign of Louis XIV*. New York: Dutton, 1966, p. 149.

37. Nancy Mitford, *The Sun King*. New York: Harper & Row, 1966, p. 38.

38. Château de Versailles, "The Hall of Mirrors." http://en.chateau versailles.fr.

39. Tony Spawforth, *Versailles: A Biography of a Palace*. New York: St. Martin's Griffin, 2008, p. 34.

40. Quoted in Spawforth, *Versailles*, p. 41.

41. Quoted in Levron, *Daily Life at Versailles in the Sixteenth and Seventeenth Centuries*, p. 76.

42. Quoted in Ziegler, *At the Court of Versailles*, p. 149.

43. Mitford, *The Sun King*, p. 96.

44. Quoted in Editors of Time-Life Books, *What Life Was Like During the Age of Reason*. Alexandria, VA: Time-Life, 1999, p. 37.

45. Quoted in Levron, *Daily Life at Versailles in the Sixteenth and Seventeenth Centuries*, p. 166.

46. Quoted in Paul R. Hanson, *The A to Z of the French Revolution*. Lanham, MD: Scarecrow, 2007, p. 314.

Chapter Five: Versailles in the Modern Era

47. Quoted in Jean-Pierre Babelon, "The Louvre: Royal Residence and Temple of the Arts," in *Realms of Memory: The Construction of the French Past*, vol. 3, ed. Pierre Nora and Lawrence D. Kritzman, trans. Arthur Goldhammer. New York: Columbia University Press, 1998, p. 278.

48. Quoted in "Versailles," *London Quarterly Review,* Vol. LXI, January, 1838, *American Edition.* New York: William Lewer, 1838, p. 6. http://books.google.com.

49. Payne, *The Story of Versailles.*

50. Spawforth, *Versailles,* p. 244.

51. Quoted in EyeWitness to History, "Signing the Treaty of Versailles, 1919." www.eyewitnesstohistory.com.

52. Quoted in Institut National d'Histoire de l'Art, "Nolhac, Pierre (de)." www.inha.fr.

53. *Time,* "Foreign News: Versailles," March 17, 1923. www.time.com.

54. Quoted in *Time,* "Art: Royal House of Cards," December 10, 1951. www.time.com.

55. Quoted in Château de Versailles, "1962–1966 André Malraux and Versailles." http://en.chateauversailles.fr.

56. Quoted in Alan Riding, "The Hall of Mirrors: Almost Good as New," *New York Times,* June 26, 2007. www.nytimes.com.

57. Quoted in Clare Garner, "French Storm Damage a 'Catastrophe,'" *Independent,* December 28, 1999. www.independent.co/uk.

58. Quoted in *USA Today,* "Storm's Destruction at Versailles Has Happy Ending," December 31, 2004. http://usatoday30.usatoday.com.

FACTS ABOUT THE PALACE OF VERSAILLES

Construction
- Time to complete construction: About 50 years
- Approximate cost to build Versailles: 116,438,892 livres (about $2 billion in today's money)

Interior Features
- Number of rooms: 2,300
- Number of windows: 2,153
- Number of staircases: 67
- Number of fireplaces: 2,252
- Number of mirrors in the Hall of Mirrors: 357
- Area of palace: 721,182 square feet (67,000 sq. m)

Exterior
- Total area of palace and gardens: 19,262 acres (7,795 ha)
- Perimeter of wall enclosing the palace and gardens: 12 miles (19.3 km)

Palace Life
- Number of residents: Up to 20,000
- Number of kings living there before the French Revolution: 4
- Number of horses in the Royal Stables: 2,000

Gardens
- Number of trees in the gardens: 200,000
- Number of fountains in the gardens: 50

Artwork
- Number of sculptures in the palace: 2,102
- Number of paintings: 6,100
- Number of engravings: 15,304
- Number of drawings: 1,500

FOR FURTHER RESEARCH

Books

James Barter, *The Palace of Versailles*. San Diego: Lucent, 1999.

Pierre L. Horn, *King Louis XIV*. New York: Chelsea House, 1986.

Anthony Mason, *Versailles*. New York: World Almanac Library, 2005.

Nancy Plain, *Louis XVI, Marie Antoinette, and the French Revolution*. Tarrytown, NY: Marshall Cavendish, 2002.

Louise Chipley Slavicek, *The Treaty of Versailles*. New York: Chelsea House, 2010.

Philip Wilkinson, *Great Buildings*. New York: DK, 2012.

Websites

Château de Versailles (en.chateauversailles.fr/homepage). As the official website of the Palace of Versailles, this site features extensive information on all aspects of the palace, its history, the people associated with it, and current activities.

Louis XIV—the Sun King (www.louis-xiv.de). This site offers information on the Sun King: a biography, his politics, his religion, and descriptions of life in the court at Versailles.

Maquettes Historiques (www.maquettes-historiques.net/P50 .html). This is the English version of a French website featuring photographs of models of Versailles and its gardens.

Splendors of Versailles (http://splendors-versailles.org). This educational website includes a teacher's guide, student supplement, and resources and activities centered around the history of Versailles.

Stockholm360, "Gallery: The Palace of Versailles" (www.stockholm
360.net/list.php?id=versailles). This website presents panoramic photographs of several rooms in the palace, including the Hall of Mirrors. This virtual tour will make visitors to the site feel as though they
are actually in the rooms.

INDEX

PICTURE CREDITS

ABOUT THE AUTHOR

Craig E. Blohm has written numerous books and magazine articles for young readers. He and his wife, Desiree, reside in Tinley Park, Illinois.